W9-BIQ-316

Breaking the
Access Barriers

Carnegie Commission on Higher Education

Publications in Print

Breaking the Access Barriers

A PROFILE OF TWO-YEAR COLLEGES

by *Leland L. Medsker*

Director, Center for Research and Development in Higher Education,
University of California, Berkeley

and *Dale Tillery*

Professor of Higher Education,
University of California, Berkeley

with a commentary by *Joseph P. Cosand*

Fourth of a Series of Profiles Sponsored by
The Carnegie Commission on Higher Education

MCGRAW-HILL BOOK COMPANY

New York   St. Louis   San Francisco   Düsseldorf
London   Sydney   Toronto   Mexico   Panama
Johannesburg   Kuala Lumpur   Montreal
New Delhi   Rio de Janeiro   Singapore

*The Carnegie Commission on Higher Education,
1947 Center Street, Berkeley, California 94704,
has sponsored preparation of this profile as a
part of a continuing effort to obtain and present
significant information for public discussion.
The views expressed are those of the authors.*

BREAKING THE ACCESS BARRIERS
A Profile of Two-Year Colleges

07-010023-3

Foreword

The uniquely American two-year colleges are called on to perform a greater variety of services for a more diverse clientele than any other category of higher education. The proof that the nation needs and values their comprehensiveness was spectacularly demonstrated in the sixties when enrollments more than doubled. They are projected to double again in the current decade, probably exceeding 4 million by 1980.

Convenience, low cost, and an open-door admissions policy make them attractive to thousands who otherwise either would not or could not consider education beyond high school. It is significant that more than half of all two-year college students are over 21 years of age. These local institutions, in addition to training young men and women for ever-changing career needs, offer traditional undergraduate academic work for transferees to four-year colleges and universities, give many young adults a second start, supply continuing education—both general and occupational—for older citizens, and serve their communities as centers of intellectual and cultural activity. Increasingly in recent years their civic role has been oriented to the various kinds of manpower needs of public agencies, as in providing out-service training for police and firemen and course offerings in the expanding health specialties.

In a sense the community colleges are expected to be nearly all things to nearly all men and women. They have succeeded remarkably well in a number of states, thriving and growing with the multiple roles thrust upon them; and in seven "pacesetter" states they have thrived spectacularly. But, unfortunately, the growth in numbers of colleges in the nation as a whole has been uneven. Many communities still lack colleges within commuting distance of those who need them.

In addition to the need for more colleges, the authors point out, it is essential that there be better planning and coordination of the two-year institutions with local secondary schools and the four-year colleges and universities in a given region.

The authors, both of whom have been deeply involved in the community college movement in the United States, share the views of the Carnegie Commission (*The Open-Door Colleges,* June, 1970) that local financial support must be supplemented increasingly by the states and the federal government. At the same time, the colleges must be left operationally free to experiment and innovate as their roles and the changing times require.

The Commission is pleased to present this profile view of the evolution of the two-year colleges and their dramatic burgeoning in recent years, along with recommendations for their future development.

Clark Kerr
Chairman
The Carnegie Commission
on Higher Education

Contents

9 *Summary, Issues, and Recommendations,* 135

1. *Introduction*

The phenomenal growth of the two-year colleges in the sixties, combined with many pressures upon them for change, has resulted in a category of uniquely American institutions that is not always well understood—either by the public or by the educational community itself. Indeed, the colleges vary so widely from state to state and from one to another that at times their only common denominator seems to be the fact that they all offer two years of postsecondary instruction.

Foreign educators, needless to say, also find it difficult to understand the diverse roles of this institution, so increasingly relied on here. They come on inspection tours from countries around the world, however, seeking to learn how or whether some version of it can be adapted abroad.

Basically, the two-year colleges are of two types: those that are publicly controlled, often referred to as community colleges, and those that are private, or independent. Both public and private institutions are sometimes called "junior colleges," and in this book the term is used interchangeably. Only the tax-supported institutions, however, are considered community colleges.

Within each category, public and private, the range of characteristics is great—an indication that the two-year colleges are working hard to serve their varied constituents. An imaginary visit to three distinctive types of campuses will give the reader an idea of their breadth and diversity.

SCENE 1:
SUBURBAN
COLLEGE

The first institution on our tour is a new and rapidly expanding college in a community adjacent to a large city. On its 200-acre campus with its commanding and slightly rolling terrain are seven modern buildings separated by comfortable distances, wide walkways, and green lawns. On one side of the landscape the framework of a building under construction gives evidence of a campus still uncompleted. Large parking lots parallel the perimeter road to the campus.

Now in its third year, the college—which is maintained by a district embracing some 15 communities—enrolls over 5,000 students, about half of whom are classified as part-time. The college day continues through evening four nights each week. During these hours many students take credit courses in both academic and vocational fields while others enroll on a noncredit basis in such subjects as gardening, travel, contemporary novel, income taxes, family financial planning, and interior design.

Since its beginning, Suburban College has been strongly oriented toward the community. It was originally conceived by thoughtful citizens in the various subcommunities within the district as a means of providing an educational opportunity for hundreds of young people who otherwise would find it difficult to continue their education beyond high school; this despite the fact that in some of the communities the socioeconomic level is reasonably high. Many of the citizens who got behind the community college idea at the outset worked vigorously in elections to bring the district into being and to gain financial support for it.

In its brief existence the college has become a source of pride for citizens throughout the district. In addition to the courses it offers for credit and noncredit it provides a host of community services such as sharing its computer services with the local public schools, providing (through its dental hygiene clinic) dental health education programs in the community, conducting business management seminars for local industries, holding community symposia for women, and making its physical facilities available to community groups. The college recently established a community counseling center which, on a fee basis, is open to individuals in the district.

An initial argument for the establishment of Suburban College was that it would prepare technicians for the rapidly growing business, industrial, and professional interests in the area. In accordance with this goal the college moved quickly to initiate both one- and two-year career programs. The two-year programs lead to the Associate Degree, and, in keeping with the idea that the career ladder should be open-ended, many credits are transferrable. The one-year programs lead to a Certificate of Completion. In fall, 1969, over 30 percent of the students were pursuing to all students. Individuals and groups in the community know that their requests for new programs or new courses will not meet with bureaucratic indifference. Administrators and faculty participate in the community, and lines of communication between school and community are short. Many programs have had their inception in the community—not through formal, fixed patterns of official procedures, but rather through the sensitive interpretation of community needs on the part of the college staff.

Training programs at Valley College were once limited to preparation for advanced study. Changing societal needs have added many vocationally oriented programs in industry and technology. Training courses for food service, police, and paramedical careers are a few examples of these new programs. Serving students' needs is the ultimate objective of this training, but indirectly it fulfills parental aspirations and develops a reservoir of skills and talents to meet the needs of a changing community.

Since Valley is part of a large community college district, bussing services and residence halls are available for students who live considerable distances from the campus. These services help to equalize the opportunity for education.

For many years the staff has been recruited on a national basis. The faculty represents various regions and educational institutions. This encourages a diversity of opinions. There is deep respect for academic freedom and a minimum of administrative direction in educational matters. Improvement of instruction is a common concern, and there is a willingness on the part of both faculty and administration to try new approaches and to accept change.

An unusual number of Valley College students remain in the community, and it follows that the alumni organization is important. Its constant campus-oriented activities and its fund-raising events for scholarships are effective and well supported. It is not uncommon to see a student rooting section of 3,500 sitting next to an alumni section of 2,000 members. Neither is it uncommon for as many as 4,000 followers to travel 125 miles to see their team in action. This welcomed community support is a logical result of the services that this institution provides for the academic, vocational, and cultural needs of the students and community.

SCENE 3:
METROPOL-
ITAN COLLEGE
We move now to Metropolitan College, which is the downtown campus of a multiunit community college district serving a highly industrialized midwestern city. Ground was broken for the present

campus in 1966 on a 40-acre site cleared some years earlier as part of an urban redevelopment project. The new campus is architecturally unique and modern. Ten large buildings now serve a student body in excess of 10,000 and may eventually house 15,000 students.

The community setting of the campus is predominantly lower-income white, with a small but rapidly growing percentage of black families. The vicinity is in a state of transition in at least two dimensions. The population is shifting in the direction of more black families, and at the same time the area is attracting service industries. In this setting, the college offers a comprehensive program in arts and sciences, careers, and community service.

All students commute, and only one-third attend full-time. Over half come from families with incomes of less than $10,000 per year. The student body has a higher-than-average age, and nearly half are enrolled in career and vocational types of programs, which is much higher than the national average.

Over half the faculty of Metropolitan are employed on a part-time basis. The college is making an effort to recruit more blacks and members of other ethnic groups for the faculty as the racial balance of the clientele changes.

The stated objectives of the institution are to serve a broad range of educational needs but especially those of the inner-city student. Some 20 career programs in business, health technology, engineering, and public service are offered by the college. As part of its community service program, it recently prepared 100 caseworkers and home service aides for the county, an equal number of municipal aides for the city, 30 educational aides for selected school districts, and 30 aides for the state employment office.

But the dynamics of a college in the inner city are the result of many factors over and beyond its general curriculum. They are determined in part by the college's physical image gained through small units working throughout its service area or through a group of buildings that form a campus. They also are centered in the types of special programs that are established with the aid of and for the poor.

The Metropolitan College campus stands as a physical symbol, but its impact depends in part on how people react to environmental changes resulting from its establishment. Since the college is located in a redevelopment area, many old buildings and homes were bulldozed away, leaving a barren plot. Many long-time residents of the area had to abandon their homes and resettle in new areas. For some time, the land remained bare and unused except for occasional sandlot football and baseball games.

From the perspective of local residents the campus today is a sight to behold: a multilevel, carefully landscaped expanse of grass, shrubs, and trees, attractively decorated with fountains, ponds, and open pathways. Many feel that because it is located on a site previously occupied by families of the community, the college belongs to them. Yet, they are unsure about using the college. They note the sharp contrast between the key features of the college and of the community. The campus is new—the community old; the campus appears rich and plush—the community is poor; the campus is modern, technological, futuristic—the community is old, static, and outmoded. Some people of the community are astounded, overwhelmed, and frustrated by the college. They are not quite sure "what's in it for them."

But steps are being taken to break the barriers. One program which touches the inner core of a major black ghetto is a comprehensive educational counseling service aimed at poor students in the several high schools served by the college. The specially trained counselors in the college work with these students to encourage them to finish high school and to continue their education. A special attempt is made to provide financial help for needy black students, whether in the high school, the local college, or in some other postsecondary institution. The director of this program is black, as are most of his staff. Offices are located in an old building in the heart of the slum and are used as a base from which counselors and staff work in the local high schools with graduating seniors.

In many ways, the events and problems at Metropolitan are symptomatic of the uncertainties created when a new campus is born in the inner city. The process of working out accommodations so that the expressed needs of urban people can be effectively met is slow and frustrating. But it is a task which this community college and many like it are assuming for the 1970s.

The three colleges we have visited are really not prototypes but instead are examples of the variety of two-year institutions that dot the country.

The private colleges are equally diverse. Some are coeducational, while others enroll either men only or women only. Some are highly sectarian in that they are closely related to either the Catholic church or to a certain denomination of the Protestant church, while others, though church-related, have a less formal association. Many are simply charted as nonprofit institutions with no ties to an outside organization. They vary in objectives, size, and breadth of curriculum, as well as in tuition and living accommodations. Students elect to attend private junior colleges for quite personal reasons — some because they consider such institutions as superior in quality and generally smaller in size than public colleges, others because of their desire to live away from home while going to school, and still others because of their connections with the church of their faith. Each private college has a personality of its own and generally a closely knit student group. It is part of an American tradition that survives even under today's difficult problems of rising costs and financial support.

Nearly 70 years have elapsed since the first public, and 120 years since the first private, junior colleges were established. Those who first advocated such institutions, as well as those who were originally responsible for their establishment, scarcely could have envisioned the extent to which their dream would be realized. With a total current enrollment of almost 2 million students, the private and public junior colleges today number over 1,000. Since the end of World War II the main thrust of the two-year-college movement has been in the public segment, and since 1961 the number of these colleges has about doubled. In many of the 50 states, the goal of planning agencies is to ensure that such a college exists within commuting distance of all high school graduates. Several states have achieved this goal.

National attention to junior colleges is increasing. They are the subject of articles in various kinds of popular, business, and professional periodicals. All the post-World War II presidents of the United States have by various means acknowledged the importance of the junior college.

Societal forces are responsible for the phenomenal growth and development of these schools. The era of the post-Industrial Revolution has, for many reasons, led to the goal of near universal educational opportunity beyond the secondary school. This, together with the recent explosion of the college-age population, has posed many problems for higher education. To meet the need, new institutions have been established and existing ones expanded. Those planning the expansion have favored decentralization, proximity to students, and economy—criteria which have caused states to turn to community colleges.

It is, however, incorrect to assume that the growth and acceptance of community colleges can be attributed only to convenience and economy. With the advent of the technological revolution and the accompanying social changes, higher education itself has undergone a process of evaluation which has placed a new reliance on unconventional structures and unconventional institutions. New manpower needs have developed, and old ones have changed. The fact that many students who, only a decade ago, would not have considered going beyond high school now tend to continue their education has led to great diversity among students and diversity among educational programs. This in turn has led to a recognized need for differences among institutions.

Their location close to the homes of potential students, their nonselective admissions policies, and their tendency to offer a variety of programs (many of which lead directly to employment rather than to a baccalaureate degree) have made community colleges the most significant of all higher institutions in extending educational opportunity. The presence of a public two-year college in a community means that a much higher proportion of high school graduates from lower socioeconomic or ability levels can continue their education than could in a community with no college at all. For some students, community colleges provide a "second chance" and, by their (presumably) nontraditional approach, a variety of programs. Such colleges now enroll a far greater number of students from groups hitherto underrepresented in higher education than do other types of colleges, and they will soon assume a decidedly more important role in this regard.

Yet the student body of most community colleges is by no means composed only of those on the lower end of the various scales. The typical community college tends to draw heavily from all quartiles of ability distribution. In terms of general background, the composition of the student body is highly representative of the community as a whole. Community colleges are also looked to by increasing numbers of adults at all levels who wish to enhance their personal or vocational competence and to do so at minimum expense without disruption of family and employment.

The versatility of the two-year college has led not only to new perceptions of higher education but to its restructuring as well. Thus, there is a trend toward the diversion of lower-division students to community colleges which is accomplished by increasing the degree of selectivity at four-year colleges, limiting their intake of freshmen, providing space for transfer students, and establishing new upper-division colleges. In the country as a whole, approximately 29 percent of all undergraduate students were in junior colleges in 1968. In some states the number of freshmen and sophomore students in two-year colleges far exceeds the number found in four-year institutions. In California in the fall of 1968, 90 community colleges accounted for 81.6 percent of all students in lower-division studies in all of the public and private higher educational institutions.

This report reviews some of the data concerning junior colleges as they assume a greater role in an evolving pattern of higher education. Our intention is to deal with the subject objectively and to consider problems, issues, and concerns as well as proclaimed attributes. If they are to assume the responsibilities in American postsecondary education that many people see for them, junior colleges obviously must be subjected to continuous examination so that the individuals and agencies responsible for local, state, and national planning can have adequate information concerning them. To this end, the report, in addition to presenting a statistical portrait of junior colleges in the United States, will deal with such problems as clientele, functions, program, control, staffing, financing, and planning. Because of differences between private and public institutions, a separate chapter will be devoted to the former and their problems. University extension centers, technical institutes, and other two-year institutions of postsecondary education will be considered briefly, primarily to examine important relationships with two-year colleges and other institutions of higher education.

2. From Expansion to Explosion

It may be hard to believe, but the facts speak for themselves: More than 50 new community colleges—an average of one per week—are established each year. In 1968 more than 1.8 million students were enrolled in 739 of these institutions. And the end is not in sight. The staff of the Carnegie Commission on Higher Education estimates that, by 1980, 3.6 to 4.3 million students will be enrolled in these colleges, and it projects the need for 230 to 280 new community colleges within a 10-year period. Such is the story of the fastest growing educational institution in the United States.

EVOLUTION OF THE TWO-YEAR COLLEGE
In retrospect, the community college movement in America began modestly, developed slowly, then surged into the twentieth century. There were a few privately controlled two-year postsecondary schools already in operation in the middle 1800s, with curricula designed primarily to provide traditional lower-division offerings. These institutions served select youth of particular religious faiths.

American public community colleges came into being near the turn of the last century, being conceived by a few innovative educators of that period as the capstone unit of an integrated system of secondary and postsecondary education. Such two-year institutions were designed to meet more effectively the new knowledge requirements of a society caught in a dramatic shift from a rural-agricultural to an urban-industrial base. Academic preparation for transfer to four-year colleges and universities was a super-ordinate function of the curriculum. In this, public colleges adhered to the prevalent concept of higher education found in the more limited but prestigious objectives of existing private colleges. But uniquely democratic factors were introduced. An industrial society required both liberal education and such professional training as engineering and business education. Moreover, population growth was reflected in the increasing number and variety of students seeking entrance to four-year institutions—particularly the newly developed land-grant state colleges—through initial admission to two-year colleges. Thus, junior colleges in the United States evolved naturally from the egalitarian premise that each individual should be allowed to develop to the limits of his capabilities.

While this concept of higher education did not gain wide acceptance at the time, by the early decades of the twentieth century it claimed an increasing number of adherents. A few local school systems began to offer work at the freshman and sophomore levels. The movement made considerable progress in the Midwest under William Rainey Harper, president of the University of Chicago, who set up a system of affiliated colleges attached to an academy or public high school. In 1911, in Fresno, California, the high school established a junior college with three teachers and 15 students, thus giving birth to what would become one of the most extensive public junior college systems in the country. Other states such as New York, Oklahoma, and Mississippi were early to establish state-supported systems of public junior colleges, primarily to provide opportunities for rural youth in still homogeneous communities removed from urban centers.

However, up to the time of World War II, private junior colleges substantially outnumbered public institutions. The public two-year college movement was yet vaguely understood, supported by only meager enrollment, and often labeled an institutional curiosity. The literature detailing its development gives little indication that it seriously threatened other forms of public education above the elementary level, or that it received more than passing attention in the communities it served. Indeed, its all-purpose effort seemed for a time to be overshadowed by the emergence of the comprehensive high school.

Occupational programs in the junior college were first developed as a result of the Smith-Hughes vocational education legislation in the 1920s and as a reaction to the pressing economic needs growing out of the Great Depression. These two events stimulated and fostered implementation of the *comprehensive* community college. Still, in that prewar period, few citizens attended junior colleges—perhaps less than 200,000 full-time students were enrolled on a national basis in 1940. These colleges were not yet perceived as part of higher education.

The public two-year college experienced phenomenal growth following World War II. Several factors were responsible. First, an
expanding job market—particularly based in the broad area of
industrial technology—required new training programs of varied
intensity and scope. Here, the measured retraining of returning
military personnel who had attended vocational schools in the
services became a highlight of the new occupational curricula.
Second, the passage of Public Law 16—the so-called G. I. Bill of
Rights—heavily augmented the enrollments of existing colleges
and universities. In the first postwar year of 1946, for example,
public and private institutions in the United States enrolled approximately one and a half million students of whom 462,000 were
returned military personnel. In the same year, community colleges
moved quickly to absorb the enrollment spill-over of crowded four-
year institutions.

Finally, the global aspect of a war recently fought on many
fronts increased the interest for enlightened, comprehensive education. Aspirations to learn more about the world and its ways as
well as the desire for occupational upgrading were reflected in
the rapid growth of continuing education programs at the community college. Adults—citizens who never before had considered
a "college" education—looked increasingly to local colleges as
community centers which could provide a wide spectrum of educational and cultural activities. Junior college total enrollment for
1946 was approximately 10 percent of the total national enrollment
for institutions of higher education—a new high.

At some point during this postwar resurgence of the two-year
college, it came to be known as the "people's college." The vague
and lingering distinctions made between postsecondary and higher
education now served only as bureaucratic conveniences for state
and local agencies of education. For the growing number of con-
sumers of varying ages and needs, such semantic niceties had little
meaning. The public two-year college now merged its parochial
efforts with those of four-year institutions to bring to the local
community the full thrust of comprehensive postsecondary education.

Since the mid-twentieth century, the pressure of new admissions
has continued to be exerted upon the community college, and an
ever-increasing number of students of all ages seek education
beyond high school. The college-age product of the post-World
War II baby boom is still substantially represented in today's

enrollment figures. Veterans of the Korean War and the Viet Nam conflict continue to enter the community college, encouraged by increasing financial support provided by state and federal legislation. And recently, minority Americans, the urban disadvantaged, and other poverty groups are demanding equal educational opportunity.

The rapid growth of the two-year college in the sixties was a response to these pressures. Commissions on higher education in both the Truman and Eisenhower administrations recognized this growth, the former noting that 50 percent of the population had capabilities for benefiting from 14 years of education. Similarly, the Eisenhower Commission held that the "expansion of the two-year college has been one of the most notable developments in post-high school education in twentieth century America." In 1960, the Commission on National Goals reinforced this awareness by predicting that in the near future the two-year college would enroll more than 50 percent of the students entering college for the first time. And in 1964, the Educational Policies Commission of the National Education Association maintained that any high school graduate must be allowed to take two years of postsecondary education if the nation's goal of universal educational opportunity is to be realized.

Viewed in the historical perspective, the public community colleges have come a long way in a very short time. It may be too soon to say they have the potential for giving the twentieth century an updated version of the American Dream—unrestricted opportunity for higher education for all citizens. Yet with a flair for brash endeavor as refreshing and inspiring as it is often abrasive, the community colleges have touched the spirit of tomorrow.

MEASURING GROWTH Chart 1 shows the impressive growth of junior college enrollments during the past 10 years in contrast to their steady growth in previous decades. The last recorded five years show a rapid increase in the number of institutions (both public and private) from 719 in 1964 to 993 in 1968. Total enrollment for this same period has also risen dramatically, by nearly 1 million students.

Numbers have thus increased by more than 100,000 each year since 1964. Nationally, an average of about one-third of all students entering a higher education program start in a junior college. For some states the figure is much greater, e.g., Illinois, 54 percent; New York, 50 percent; Florida, 69 percent; California, 80 percent.

CHART 1
*Enrollment in
two-year
colleges,
United States,
1930–1970*

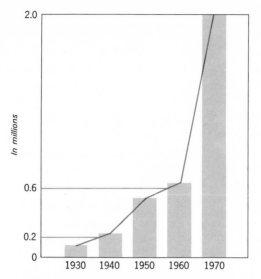

SOURCE: Adapted from American Council on Education data, with estimated 1970 enrollments.

Today, the community junior college national enrollment — approximately 2 million students — is nearly 28 percent of the total undergraduate enrollment in higher education in the United States.[1] A large and heterogeneous student consumer group seems a natural response to an educational enterprise which features low cost, residential proximity, flexible admission arrangements, and a varied educational program to suit the needs of the time.

Numbers of Colleges

While Chart 2 indicates consistent total overall growth for junior colleges, it should be noted that this growth pattern emphasized the development of the public institutions. The number of public two-year colleges has nearly doubled in a decade — from 656 to over 1,100 in 1970. In the same period, however, there was a decline in the number of nonpublic junior colleges.

Enrollment

The increase in student enrollment in public community colleges has been equally spectacular, as shown in Chart 3. Combined full-time and part-time enrollment for these institutions in 1958

[1] Although Charts 1 and 4 are adapted from American Association of Junior Colleges and American Council on Education reports, resulting in a higher but more realistic reporting of enrollments, these particular data are derived for the purpose of consistency from 1968 U.S. Office of Education reports of opening fall enrollments in higher education.

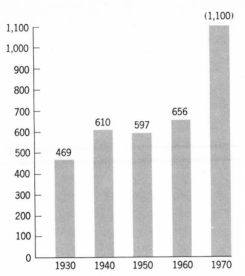

SOURCE: Adapted from American Council on Education data with estimated number of junior colleges in 1970.

totaled 374,672. By 1968, that combined figure had increased almost 400 percent to approximately 1,811,000. A more meaningful picture of enrollment growth in public colleges can be gained from a diachronic comparison of full-time with part-time groupings. Chart 3 shows that both categories of student enrollment have increased substantially since 1958—by 530 percent for part-time students and 340 percent for full-time students in 1967.

Until 1965, part-time students outnumbered their full-time counterparts by an annual average of approximately 55,000, although the gross number of students separating the groups had been decreasing steadily. Then, in 1966, full-time enrollment for the first time surpassed by 38,000 the number of part-time students. The modest reversal of form appears to be a consistent trend.

Again, these general growth data can be understood to measure the serious response by a public increasingly aware of the need for acquiring skills and knowledge in a complex society. They probably attest also to the growing popularity of a local public institution of higher education which can fill that need promptly and at nominal cost. While variables contributing generally to such growth are discussed at length elsewhere in this report, the

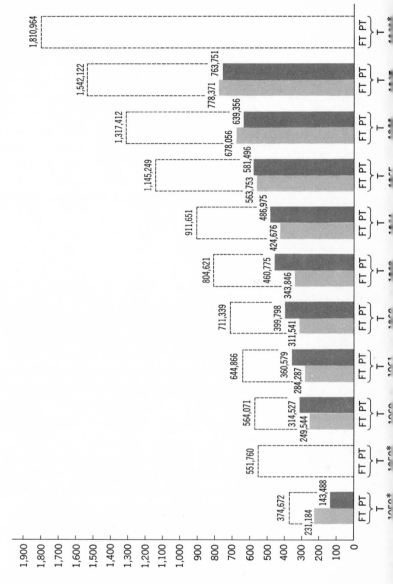

CHART 3
Comparison of full- and part-time public community college enrollments, 1958–1968

*Figures for 1958 approximate because of different reporting system in use prior to 1960. Figures for 1959 were not broken down into full- and part-time. Figures for 1968 are gross as full- and part-time breakdown was not available at time of publication.

SOURCE: American Association of Junior Colleges annual directories.

trend toward increased full-time enrollment is undoubtedly explained in major part by the gradual contraction of traditional part-time and extended program offerings in public community colleges throughout the nation. However, it would be intriguing to consider a secondary, but surely timely, explanation here.

Between 1958 and 1968, technological and skilled manpower needs in effect mandated the expansion of community college curricula. Not only was the number of postsecondary institutions increased to accommodate additional students seeking the new learning, but new programs were developed. Usually for budgetary reasons, this often meant that requisite programs could begin only as pilot offerings or on a part-time basis. Literally thousands of programs were initiated in this manner in the 1960s. When such programs became firmly established, leading to associate degree programs, they attracted full-time students.

As a result of the Vocational Education Act of 1963 and other enabling federal career legislation passed in the mid-1960s, massive financial support was given to the development of the widest array of occupational training programs in the history of public community college education. Again, Chart 3 suggests that the eventual surpassing in 1966 of the national part-time enrollment by full-time enrollment may be explained partly by recent heavy matriculation into fully developed and operational career training programs.

Figures in Chart 4 show opening fall enrollments for all degree-credit students. Since the mid-1960s, the upsurge has been marked in the numbers of students enrolled in programs which are creditable toward the baccalaureate degree. In 1968, approximately one-fifth of degree-credit enrollments were in the two-year colleges. Chart 4 also shows the distribution of men and women in such programs. The ratio of male to female students in two-year colleges has remained nearly 2 to 1 over the past decade.

The 273 nonpublic colleges that existed in 1960 enrolled 93,992 students. Although the number of institutions decreased to 260, the student enrollment reached a high of 147,119 in 1966. Since then, there has been a decline in both the number of nonpublic institutions and their collective student enrollments—to 143,152 students attending 254 colleges in 1968. Nonpublic junior colleges today comprise about 25 percent of the total number of two-year colleges in the United States and enroll somewhat less than 15 percent of the students in this type of institution. Although many factors may account for the recent drop both in numbers of non-

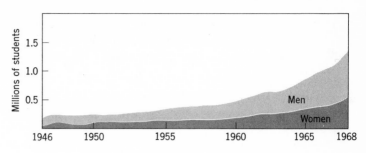

CHART 4
Junior college opening fall enrollments: all students in programs normally credited toward a baccalaureate degree

	Percent distribution	
Year	*Men*	*Women*
1960	62	38
1961	62	38
1962	62	38
1963	62	38
1964	62	38
1965	62	38
1966	61	39
1967	61	39
1968	61	39

SOURCE: American Council on Education.

public two-year colleges and in their overall enrollment, the basic problem has been and continues to be the inadequacies of economic support.

Size of Public Community Colleges

Table 1 briefly describes the distribution of enrollment in public and private junior colleges. Over 30 percent of the colleges enrolled fewer than 500 students in 1968. While the majority of the 130 public institutions may be considered developing institutions, it is not clear how such limited student enrollment can support a viable, comprehensive college operation. One hundred and ninety-eight community colleges (26.8 percent) range in size from 1,000 to 2,000 students. This is the largest size group in the overall distribution. The median enrollment is 1,380 students in public community colleges and 471 in the private colleges. There are few institutions with more than 5,000 students, and still fewer colleges have enrollments larger than 8,000. The rather considerable number of public colleges beyond 10,000 enrollment probably represents sizable central city institutions which serve a large and heterogeneous urban population.

TABLE 1	Enrollment*	Total	Public	Private
	Total institutions			
	Number	993	739	254
	Percent	100.0	100.0	100.0
	1–199	9.9	2.8	30.3
	200–499	20.9	14.7	35.4
	500–999	21.8	21.8	21.7
	1,000–1,999	22.2	26.8	8.7
	2,000–4,999	16.4	21.0	3.1
	5,000–9,999	6.3	8.3	0.8
	10,000 or more	3.4	4.6	
	Median enrollment	965	1,380	471

Public and private junior colleges by enrollment in 1968

*Includes all full-time and part-time students.

SOURCE: American Association of Junior Colleges, *1969 Junior College Directory,* Washington, D.C., 1969, p. 77. The total number of institutions is somewhat smaller than the number based on U.S. Office of Education data.

Geographic Distribution

The geographic development of community colleges in the United States has been very uneven and heavily concentrated in relatively few states, as shown in Map 1. Nevertheless, all the 50 states have public two-year colleges. Seven states (California, New York, Illinois, Michigan, Florida, Texas, and Washington) accounted for more than two-thirds of all enrollments in 1968 and over one-third of all public community colleges. In addition to these pace-setter states, there are 14 in which substantial development has taken place: Arizona, Georgia, Iowa, Kansas, Maryland, Massachusetts, Mississippi, Missouri, North Carolina, Ohio, Oregon, Pennsylvania, Virginia, and Wyoming. The remaining states fall into two groups: approximately 16 which have made a start in community college development, and another dozen where little has been done toward the development of public two-year colleges.

These state differences appear markedly in Table 2 and Map 1, which give the percentage of total undergraduate enrollments in two-year institutions by state.

A summation of the regional distribution of public community colleges is shown in Table 3. The major shifts in the American population since the early 1950s to seaboard states and to great urban centers have pushed several states to the front in community college development. Illinois and Michigan lead the Midwestern states in numbers of public colleges and enrollments, while New York and Pennsylvania in the Northeast, and Florida, North Caro-

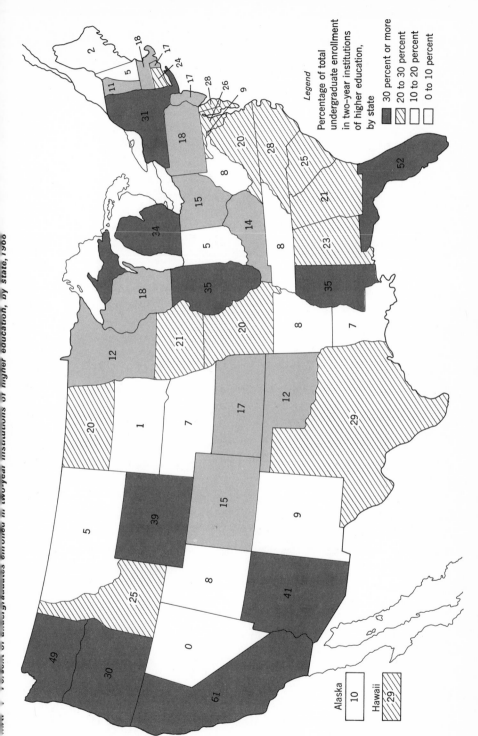

Percent of undergraduates enrolled in two-year institutions of higher education, by state, 1968

Legend

Percentage of total undergraduate enrollment in two-year institutions of higher education, by state

- 30 percent or more
- 20 to 30 percent
- 10 to 20 percent
- 0 to 10 percent

Alaska 10

Hawaii 29

SOURCE: *The Open-Door Colleges*, Carnegie Commission on Higher Education, Berkeley, June 1970.

State	Percent
TABLE 2 *Enrollment in two-year institutions of higher education as a percentage of total undergraduate enrollment, by state, 1968*	

State	Percent
Very high (30 percent or more)	
California	61.2
Florida	52.0
Washington	48.6
Arizona	41.3
Wyoming	39.4
Illinois	35.0
Mississippi	34.7
Michigan	34.2
New York	30.5
Oregon	30.4
High (20 to 30 percent)	
Hawaii	29.2
Texas	28.7
North Carolina	28.1
Delaware	27.8
Maryland	25.5
Idaho	25.2
South Carolina	25.1
Connecticut	23.9
Alabama	22.8
Iowa	20.7
Georgia	20.6
Virginia	20.4
Missouri	20.2
Moderate (10 to 20 percent)	
North Dakota	19.9
Massachusetts	18.4
Pennsylvania	17.8
Wisconsin	17.7
New Jersey	17.2
Kansas	17.1
Rhode Island	16.7
Colorado	15.0
Ohio	14.6
Kentucky	14.3
Minnesota	12.2
Oklahoma	11.7
Vermont	11.2
Low (less than 10 percent)	
Alaska	9.7
District of Columbia	9.0
New Mexico	9.0
Tennessee	8.3
Arkansas	7.9
Utah	7.9
West Virginia	7.8
Nebraska	6.7
Louisiana	6.6
Indiana	5.1

State	Percent
Montana	5.0
New Hampshire	4.9
Maine	1.6
South Dakota	1.3
Nevada	0.0

SOURCE: U.S. Office of Education data, adjusted by the staff of the Carnegie Commission on Higher Education.

lina, and Mississippi in the South account for the greatest enrollments and numbers of public colleges in those regions. In the Southwest, Texas is preeminent with its development of 42 public institutions serving nearly 80,000 students.

Private institutions are concentrated, for the most part, in the Eastern and Southern sections of the country. The greatest enrollments and numbers of nonpublic colleges for the Eastern region are found in New York and Massachusetts, with combined 1968 figures showing 38 schools and 23,314 students. The heaviest concentration in the South in 1968 was in North Carolina and Virginia, with 13,694 students and 28 institutions between them.

PACESETTER STATES Through a favorable synthesis of enabling legislation, flexible fiscal policy, and broad public support, some states have been able to develop public community college systems into impressive models for the rest of the nation. As noted earlier, seven states appear to have emerged as leaders. Of 739 public two-year colleges nationwide, these seven states have 286, of which 85 have opened since 1960. To be sure, there are other state systems which pres-

TABLE 3
Regional distribution of public community colleges, 1968

Region	Number	Percent
United States	698	100.0
New England	29	4.1
Middle Atlantic	106	15.1
Southeast	138	19.8
Southwest	56	8.0
East North Central	117	16.8
West North Central	82	11.7
Mountain	37	5.3
Pacific	133	19.0

SOURCE: Carnegie Commission on Higher Education.

TABLE 4   *Community colleges: pacesetter states*

State	Number of public community colleges 1960	1967	Total enrollments, 1967	Average size of enrollments, each college	Total 18- to 24-year-old population in state, 1967	Percent 18- to 24-year-old population served
California	67	87	540,920	6,000	2,179,000	25
Florida	25	27	81,259	3,010	652,000	13
Illinois	22	41	84,911	1,060	1,060,000	9
Michigan	16	28	79,817	2,850	870,000	9
New York	25	39	132,671	3,400	1,811,000	8
Texas	34	42	77,276	1,840	1,334,000	6
Washington	12	22	68,003	3,100	350,000	19

SOURCE: American Association of Junior Colleges and American Council on Education *Fact Book.*

ently are making rapid progress. But in the pacesetter states there has been dramatic growth of community colleges and student enrollment in the past decade. For the pacesetter states, Table 4 records the growth in number of public community colleges between 1960 and 1967, the average size of college enrollments, the college-age population in 1967, and the percent of that population served by the community colleges.

The public community college system of California now has nearly 100 institutions and leads the rest of the nation in enroll-

CHART 5
Relative growth of community college enrollments, 1960–1968, for seven pacesetter states

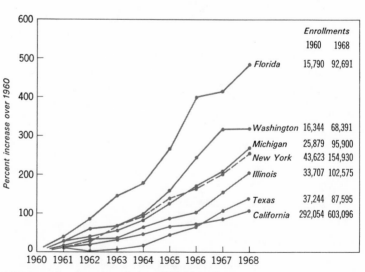

SOURCE: American Association of Junior Colleges.

ment. With Washington and Texas, it accounts for almost two-thirds of all public two-year institutions west of the Mississippi.

Public two-year college enrollment in each of these pacesetter states has increased at such a dynamic pace that their total enrollment in 1967 was well over 1 million, while in all other states combined—including the Canal Zone and Puerto Rico—the total enrollment was less than ½ million for that year. Chart 5 illustrates the enrollment growth pattern from 1960 to 1968 for seven states.

A LOOK INTO THE FUTURE As has been pointed out, the recent explosion in junior college enrollments has been largely confined to the pacesetter states (Chart 5). For the country as a whole, there has been a steady annual rise of about 1 percent in the proportion of total undergraduates attending junior colleges. It is anticipated that this rate of shift from four- to two-year institutions will continue during the coming decade. The consequences of this quiet revolution are indeed staggering to contemplate. Chart 6 shows that whereas less than one-fifth of undergraduates were in junior colleges in 1955, it is likely that by 1980 over one-third of such undergraduates will be attending two-year colleges. It is important to note that these data and those discussed below include enrollments from two-year extension centers.

Because nearly one-third of junior college students are not enrolled in programs creditable toward a bachelor's degree, projections of junior college growth are most useful when they take into

CHART 6
Observed and projected ratios of junior college enrollments to total undergraduate enrollments

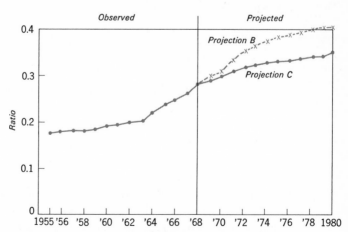

SOURCE: Adapted from the working papers of Gus Haggstrom for the Carnegie Commission on Higher Education. Projected ratios are based on enrollment projections B and C as discussed on page 28.

consideration total numbers of students who are likely to attend these institutions. In cooperation with the authors, the Carnegie Commission on Higher Education (June, 1970, pp. 33, 34) has developed several projections of enrollments in two-year institutions of higher education to 1980, based on alternative assumptions. The three sets of projections of total enrollments, including full-time and part-time students, are based upon past trends in each state's undergraduate enrollment rates relative to the number of high school graduates in that state during the preceding four years. The three projections — A, B, and C — of two-year college enrollments for each state include enrollments for two-year branches of universities and are based on the following assumptions about the future relationship between two-year college enrollment and total undergraduate enrollment:

For Projection A, the assumption is that the proportion of undergraduates in the two-year colleges will remain the same as that in 1968 (29 percent).

For Projection B, it is assumed that 60 percent of the future growth in undergraduate enrollment will be absorbed in two-year colleges. (This 60 percent figure has been exceeded in four states during the past five-year period.)

For Projection C, it is assumed that the future annual increase in percentage of undergraduate enrollment in the two-year colleges in each state will be the same as that estimated for each state from data for the past five-year period. According to Projection C, the proportion of undergraduates enrolled in the two-year colleges, including two-year branches of universities, will rise from 29 percent in the United States in 1968 to about 35 percent in 1980.

The three projections of total two-year college enrollment shown in Table 6 range from about 3,100,000 to 4,400,000 in 1980. The assumptions underlying Projection B are probably realistic only for states with 30 percent or more of undergraduates enrolled in two-year colleges in 1968 and for most of those with 20 to 30 percent in two-year colleges (Table 5 and Map 1). Projection C is more realistic for the remaining states. If there are decisive state and national efforts to stimulate community college development, enrollments will increase more rapidly than those suggested by Projection C. Nevertheless, this more conservative of the two projections shown in Table 5 is the one used in this book unless otherwise specified.

	Number		Percent of undergraduate enrollment		Percent of total enrollment	
Year	Projection B	Projection C	B	C	B	C
1968	1,871,000	1,871,000	29	29	25	25
1975	3,560,000	3,110,000	38	33	32	28
1980	4,430,000	3,740,000	41	35	34	28
1985	4,280,000	3,610,000	42	35	33	27
1990	4,380,000	3,690,000	42	35	33	28
1995	5,340,000	4,400,000	44	36	35	29
2000	6,620,000	5,340,000	46	37	36	29

TABLE 5 Enrollment in two-year institutions of higher education, actual, 1968, and projections to 2000, in numbers and as a percentage of total undergraduate enrollment and total enrollment in higher education

SOURCE: Carnegie Commission on Higher Education.

Both projections show a rapid rise in the proportion of total undergraduates enrolled in two-year colleges until 1980 and a slower increase after that, as the number of young people in the population declines. However, demographic factors may be less important in determining community college enrollments than those of other institutions of higher education. This seems likely because adults represent about half of all two-year college students, and therefore total enrollments in these institutions might go on increasing even though enrollment of young people in the 18 to 21 age group may decline.

In examining the projections by state in Table 6, it is important to recall the differences among states in present levels of junior college development and to bear in mind that new types of educational experiences beyond high school may in the future attract students who might otherwise enroll in community colleges. For these and other reasons associated with the difficulties in projecting state enrollments, it is important that careful reevaluation of enrollment trends be made every five years or so.

For planning purposes, it is useful to have projections in terms of full-time-equivalent (FTE) enrollment. Such projections were used in Chapter 6, for example, to estimate the faculty and other staff members needed by 1975 and by 1980. There were 1,290,000 FTE enrollments in 1968, or 69 percent of total two-year college enrollment. Table 7 shows, for Projection C, FTE enrollments of 2,136,000 by 1975 and 2,570,000 by 1980.

TABLE 6 *Two-year college enrollment, actual, 1968, and three alternative projections to 1980 by state (numbers in thousands)*

State	Actual, 1968*	Projected, 1980			Percentage change, 1968–1980		
		A	B	C	A	B	C
Alabama	19.9	38.4	68.7	62.2	93.0	245.2	212.6
Alaska	0.7	1.6	6.6	1.3	128.6	842.9	85.7
Arizona	32.1	66.5	82.0	81.9	107.2	155.5	155.1
Arkansas	3.8	6.5	24.6	8.0	71.1	547.4	110.5
California	600.8	989.0	981.2	1,022.4	64.6	63.3	70.2
Colorado	13.2	23.6	55.0	32.1	78.8	316.7	143.2
Connecticut	20.4	37.4	63.0	53.5	83.3	208.8	162.3
Delaware	4.5	8.5	13.2	10.3	88.9	193.3	128.9
District of Columbia	3.9	4.1	5.7	4.3	5.1	46.2	10.3
Florida	95.4	201.1	217.3	225.0	110.8	127.8	135.8
Georgia	19.6	37.3	71.0	44.8	90.3	262.2	128.6
Hawaii	6.3	11.3	16.6	13.3	79.4	163.5	111.1
Idaho	6.6	10.8	16.5	8.9	63.6	150.0	34.8
Illinois	113.7	183.9	234.1	219.7	61.7	105.9	93.2
Indiana	7.4†	11.3	53.2	15.1	52.7	618.9	104.1
Iowa	18.9	27.2	42.9	36.0	43.9	127.0	90.5
Kansas	14.1	20.4	36.2	24.0	44.7	156.7	70.2
Kentucky	11.9	20.2	46.5	25.9	69.7	290.8	117.6
Louisiana	6.6	11.5	51.4	22.0	74.2	678.8	233.3
Maine	0.4	0.6	8.0	0.7	50.0	1,900.0	75.0
Maryland	27.1	50.6	82.3	68.2	86.7	203.7	151.7
Massachusetts	40.2	62.2	111.7	75.1	54.7	177.9	86.8
Michigan	99.7	157.5	201.1	196.3	58.0	101.7	96.9
Minnesota	16.3	25.0	59.4	36.1	53.4	264.4	121.5
Mississippi	22.0	38.4	50.4	41.6	74.5	129.1	89.1
Missouri	28.6	45.5	78.7	50.0	59.1	175.2	74.8
Montana	1.2	1.9	10.0	3.1	58.3	733.3	158.3
Nebraska	3.6	5.4	19.6	6.8	50.0	444.4	88.9
Nevada	0.0	0.0	6.3	0.0	0.0	‡	0.0
New Hampshire	1.2	2.1	11.6	2.7	75.0	866.7	125.0
New Jersey	24.2	42.7	88.7	78.3	76.4	266.5	223.6
New Mexico	3.0	6.0	23.1	9.0	100.0	670.0	200.0
New York	168.0	270.7	370.2	337.4	61.1	120.4	100.8

State	Actual, 1968*	Projected, 1980			Percentage change, 1968–1980		
		A	B	C	A	B	C
North Carolina	37.4	65.4	97.0	91.4	74.9	159.4	144.4
North Dakota	5.0	7.5	12.4	7.9	50.0	148.0	58.0
Ohio	43.3	67.4	142.3	96.4	55.7	228.6	122.6
Oklahoma	10.9	16.1	37.6	16.8	47.7	245.0	54.1
Oregon	25.1	37.9	50.3	53.6	50.1	100.4	113.5
Pennsylvania	56.1	84.5	151.8	120.3	50.6	170.6	114.4
Rhode Island	5.7	9.1	18.0	14.9	59.6	215.8	161.4
South Carolina	13.1	21.9	34.2	30.6	67.2	161.1	133.6
South Dakota	0.3	0.5	8.7	0.6	66.7	2,800.0	100.0
Tennessee	9.0	14.9	51.6	24.2	65.6	473.3	168.9
Texas	97.0	167.4	244.3	222.1	72.6	151.9	129.0
Utah	4.9	8.3	30.8	10.5	69.4	528.6	114.3
Vermont	1.9	2.7	6.5	2.6	42.1	242.1	36.8
Virginia	22.7	42.4	80.8	70.3	86.8	255.9	209.7
Washington	66.8	101.6	109.7	123.3	52.1	64.2	84.6
West Virginia	4.2	6.0	17.9	6.1	42.9	326.2	45.2
Wisconsin	27.1	45.0	87.6	53.2	66.1	223.2	96.3
Wyoming	4.8	7.9	9.6	8.4	64.6	100.0	75.0
United States	1,871.0	3,102.3	4,428.1	3,738.1	65.8	136.7	99.8

*1968 enrollments, which include both degree-credit and non-degree-credit enrollments, are based on U.S. Office of Education data; enrollments on two-year campuses of public four-year institutions are not included in OE data, but have been added. There were 78,700 students enrolled on these two-year campuses in 1968.

† Does not include four predominantly two-year branch campuses of Purdue University.

‡ Computation of a percentage increase is not meaningful when the base is zero.

SOURCE: Projections prepared by the staff of the Carnegie Commission on Higher Education, under the direction of Gus W. Haggstrom.

TABLE 7 Two-year college full-time-equivalent enrollment, actual, 1968, and projections for 1975 and 1980 (in millions)	FTE enrollments	1968	1975	1980
	Actual	1,285.5		
	Projection			
	B		2,449.5	3,043.2
	C		2,135.5	2,569.0

SOURCE: Projections prepared by the staff of the Carnegie Commission on Higher Education.

**The Need for
New Colleges**   If there is to be a community college within commuting distance
of every potential student, except in sparsely populated areas,
new colleges will have to be established in all but three states and
at a national rate during the 1970s paralleling that of the previous
decade. This would mean that new campuses would open at the
rate of about one each week unless the two-year branch campuses
of public universities in several states develop truly comprehensive
curricula. In the unlikely event that these extension centers develop
programs to serve the broad educational needs of youth and adults
at low cost, only 230 to 280 new colleges will be needed. This is
the number of new community colleges which the Carnegie Commission has called for in its special report on recommendations
for the open-door colleges. The Commission based its recommendations regarding enrollments on Projections B and C, Table 6; on
its study to identify sizable communities in which there is no public
two-year college; and on projections of average enrollments in
public two-year institutions by state. Although the Commission
believes the maximum practicable size of community colleges to
be 5,000 (day enrollments), several states already exceed that
average size, and some have policies calling for even larger institutions. On the other hand, some colleges in sparsely populated areas
may not be able to reach the minimum size of 2,000 day students
as advocated by the Commission. These state differences are
reflected in the Commission's estimates of needed new community
colleges by 1980 (Map 2).

Preliminary work on economies of scale suggests that there may
be reductions in cost per student with increased size, leveling at
about 5,000 total enrollment. Some loss of economy seems to
result as colleges grow beyond this size, probably because large
institutions tend to add expensive programs. There may, however,
be some economies again as colleges grow very large—12,000
students or more.

Educational as well as economic arguments have influenced
criteria of institutional size in two-year colleges. In order to maxi-
mize personal contact with students and to ensure responsiveness
to local communities, junior college districts have tended to develop
several campuses of modest size, ranging from 2,000 to 5,000
students. On the other hand, new ways of organizing the college
program and new ideas about campus design suggest that even
very large campuses may ensure close student-faculty relationships
and effective staff communication. The trend is clearly toward

MAP 2 . *Number of existing public two-year institutions of higher education, 1968; estimated needs for new public community colleges, 1980, by state*

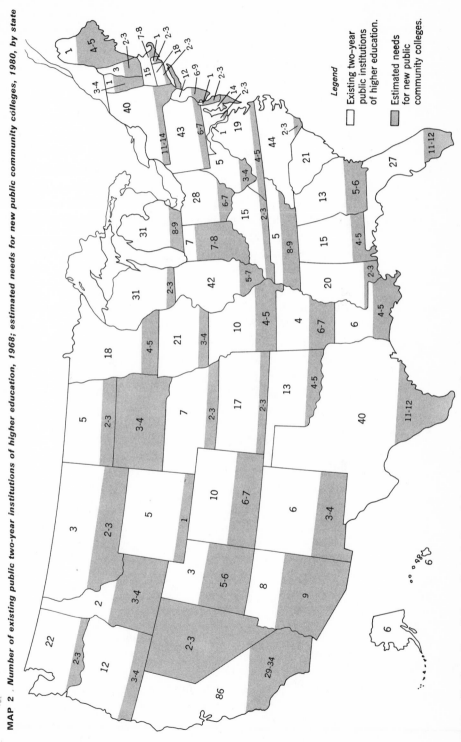

Legend

☐ Existing two-year public institutions of higher education.

⬛ Estimated needs for new public community colleges.

SOURCE: *The Open Door Colleges*, Carnegie Commission on Higher Education, Berkeley, June 1970.

larger size, and some new junior colleges are now opening their doors for the first time to 5,000 or more students.

Planning for the development of entirely new colleges is only part of the challenge ahead. Existing institutions will grow in size in order to accommodate, along with new colleges, the anticipated enrollments. In brief, facilities will be needed for at least an additional 1 million full-time-equivalent students in the 1970s.

NEW COLLEGE CAMPUSES

A visitor to America tends to be more aware of the development of junior colleges than the average citizen. As he travels the highways and byways from coast to coast, he sees stunning new campuses in the heart of cities, in the new suburbs, among the redwood forests, and in the deserts of the Southwest. Visually it is an unparalleled display of expanding educational opportunity and creativity for the development of human potential of many sorts. To be sure, not all of these new colleges have developed elaborate facilities. Some have converted older schools, industrial plants, and even department stores to suit their educational needs and limited resources. Nevertheless, the majority of the new junior colleges have been in the forefront of the most dramatic and innovative periods in the creation of educational environments.

The design process is well described by a leader in environmental design (Van Der Ryn, 1969, pp. 1–13):

Despite fancy techniques of data processing and cost benefit analysis, the physical design of (colleges) remains pretty much a process of fitting people and functions to predetermined spacial layouts. Like a housewife arranging furniture, presidents, chancellors, trustees, and their advisors go about the business of making everything fit.

Such plans, with their neatly-colored maps and artists' conceptions of grand vistas through the campus, are well suited to quick decisions by busy trustees unaccustomed to the rich diversity of activities on the real life campus.

Like other environmental designers and an increasing number of educators, Van Der Ryn observes that buildings outlive people and that much of what has been done may be obsolete in the near future. To be sure, there are many new concrete barriers to effective education, but many community college leaders, with the full involvement of their faculties and community representatives, have worked with architectural teams to anticipate the future. This enterprise has been facilitated by the American Association of Junior Colleges, the Educational Facilities Laboratory, and university centers. These efforts have given attention to definition of the community college program, effective coordination among related functions, and priority to some of the neglected needs of faculty and students.

The most recent status report on the Facilities Development Project of the American Association of Junior Colleges describes an impressive array of development activities to serve the two-year colleges (Hooker, 1969). These activities envision facilities planning as "a blending of advanced ideas about education, environment, economy, and equalization of educational opportunity" (Theodorus, 1968, p. 19). The importance of this new concern for creating environments will permit the community college to do its thing in the coming decade.

3. Junior College Students

The decade of the 1960s witnessed unprecedented interest in junior college students, especially those in public institutions. Perhaps they have been the subject of more inquiry than any other component of the two-year college, with individual junior colleges seeking information about their clientele, and outside researchers investigating who attends and why. In addition, the rapid enrollment increase and open-door nature of the public community college have led professional educators and laymen to express various opinions about the nature of the student body.

With the accumulating research findings, it is possible to view junior college students more objectively and make certain generalizations about them. This possibility, however, has also led to the danger of overcharacterization and a tendency to view "the junior college student" as if he were a prototype. The data and comments on students presented here are, for the most part, a synthesis of research findings from many sources. While they largely pertain to the public community college, they include some information about students in independent colleges. Certain comparisons are also made between students in junior colleges and those in four-year institutions.

STUDENT DIVERSITY The public community college attracts students from almost all levels of academic ability, achievement, family background, and motivation. The findings from the SCOPE[1] study conducted by Tillery et al. (1966) on a large sample of 1966 high school graduates in California, Illinois, Massachusetts, and North Carolina (each state represented a different stage in the development of community colleges) are revealing. Information was obtained about these high

---

[1] *School to College: Opportunities for Postsecondary Education.*

	Academic ability quartiles				Intellectual predisposition quartiles			
	Highest	*Above average*	*Below average*	*Lowest*	*Highest*	*Above average*	*Below average*	*Lowest*
Public and private junior colleges								
California	21	29	32	18	28	27	27	19
Illinois	29	31	28	12	26	26	29	20
Massachusetts	20	38	32	11	20	29	32	19
North Carolina	11	31	37	22	14	25	35	26
All four states: public junior colleges only	19	30	32	18	24	26	30	21
All four states: public and private junior colleges	20	31	32	17	23	27	30	21

TABLE 8 *Distribution by categories of 1966 high school graduates in four states who entered junior colleges, in percents**

*Due to rounding, the figures do not always add to 100.

NOTE: Levels are based on percentages of students in entire sample who went to college for each of the four clusters of fathers' occupations. The percentages of students from each occupational cluster who attended college were as follows: very high, 73%; high, 62%; moderate, 46%, low, 35%.

SOURCE: SCOPE Project, Center for Research and Development in Higher Education, University of California, Berkeley.

school seniors' academic ability, self-estimation of high school grade-point averages, intellectual predisposition as measured by certain scales derived from the Omnibus Personality Inventory, family occupational level, and other factors indicating student and family motivation with regard to education beyond high school.

Table 8 summarizes the distribution on the first four categories of more than 6,600 graduates in the sample who entered two-year colleges. It should be noted that composite data for all four states are reported for the graduates who entered public two-year colleges only, and for the group that entered junior colleges regardless of whether public or private.

The distributions show that diversity does indeed characterize the students entering two-year colleges despite the fact that there are differences among the four states. Two-year colleges drew substantially from all quartiles of ability, with nearly one-fifth of

Self-estimation of grade point average		Family occupational level			
Above average	*Average and below*	*Very high*	*High*	*Moderate*	*Low*
46	54	27	29	32	13
44	57	17	23	36	25
36	64	18	26	32	24
35	65	16	29	33	22
41	59	21	26	34	19
41	59	21	27	33	19

the students representing both the highest and lowest quartiles. The same was true of intellectual predisposition except that, contrary to popular belief, nearly one-fourth of the two-year college students came from the highest quartile. The fact that two-year colleges drew almost equally from all four levels indicates that, while some of their students come with a high intellectual orientation, others are very practical and are not prone to be challenged by abstract ideas and new values.

A much higher percentage of the students who entered two-year colleges came from the group of graduates who estimated their probable high school grades as average or below (59 percent) than from the group that estimated their performance as above average (41 percent). Interestingly enough, in the entire group of graduates the division was almost exactly the reverse, with 60 percent estimating they would rank excellent or good and 40 percent predicting that their grades would be average or below. State differences are significant. The California and Illinois two-year colleges attracted more students from the above average group and fewer from the lower groups, whereas in Massachusetts and North Carolina two-thirds of the two-year students were from the lower group.

In contrast, the pattern in which students from family occupational levels selected junior colleges was fairly congruent with the distribution of the entire sample: very high, 21 percent; high, 27 percent; moderate, 33 percent; and low, 19 percent. The sample is based on the percentage of the high school graduates who went to college from each of four clusters of fathers' occupations. While the percentages from these groups who went to junior colleges are not exactly the same as those for the total sample of high school graduates, they are so close as to document the tendency of two-year college students to represent the total population on most indices of socioeconomic level.

In North Carolina, except for family occupational level, a higher percentage of students in the low categories went to two-year colleges than was true in the other states. In Illinois and Massachusetts the relatively small proportion of students in these colleges who are from the lowest ability quartile may reflect the fact that the development of public junior colleges in those states has only recently been accelerated, hence it may not yet be traditional for less able students to go to college. The relatively large proportion of California students from the very high family occupational level who went to community colleges indicates the public's acceptance of these colleges in a state where they are fully developed and where the public four-year institutions are highly selective.

The four-state study also provided two indices of education aspirations. For example, of those entering two-year colleges 13 percent had indicated while in high school that they were ambitious to go *beyond* a four-year college degree, 41 percent had indicated their ambition to obtain a four-year degree, only 25 percent had chosen the junior college as their top goal, and nearly 19 percent had indicated their intention either to obtain vocational skills or not go beyond high school. In contrast, smaller percentages of their parents were interested in their children's continuing their education beyond the baccalaureate or settling for some vocational education. Many more (49 percent) indicated their desire for their children merely to obtain a baccalaureate, or (36 percent) to get "some college." These reported aspirations of both students and parents are in harmony with data from many other studies which reveal the large proportion of entering junior college students who declare their intention to transfer. Since it has been shown repeatedly that only about half of those expecting to transfer ever do so, the unrealistic expectations of many students give rise to problems for the junior college. The data reported above also show, however, that many students do indeed look to the junior college as a means of continuing their education but not as a route to a baccalaureate degree.

In an earlier study of 10,000 high school graduates in 16 communities, Medsker and Trent (1965) also assessed the distribution of characteristics of the more than 1,200 who entered a public two-year college. The distribution in terms of academic ability and by rank in high school class is reported in Table 9. Again, the relatively equal spread of both ability and high school achievement among junior college students is apparent. The study also revealed great diversity among junior college students in terms of socioeconomic background, parents' educational attainment, interests in music and literature, type of curriculum followed in high school, and the amount of discussion with parents concerning college attendance.

Reports from other studies add to the realization that students tend to be representative of the total population of their communities. Although various ethnic groups are underrepresented, in many ways the student bodies in community colleges resemble the high school populations from which most of them have just emerged. To this there are two exceptions. One is that women, who constitute only about 40 percent of the enrollment, are still underrepresented in the community college. The other is that many community college students are much older than recent high school graduates. The age distribution varies by institution and also according to the times, but, generally speaking, over 30 percent of community college freshmen are 20 years of age or older; some of them well along in years. And if evening part-time students are included, the median age is well above that of the college population group.

TABLE 9
Distribution of academic ability and class rank of high school graduates entering public two-year colleges

	Quintiles						
	I (High)	*II*	*III*	*IV*	*V* (Low)	*Not available*	*Total*
Academic ability	24	20	20	16	17	3	100
Rank in high school class	21	21	20	15	11	12	100

SOURCE: Extracted from Leland L. Medsker and James W. Trent, *The Influence of Different Types of Public Higher Institutions on College Attendance from Varying Socioeconomic and Ability Levels,* Center for Research and Development in Higher Education, University of California, Berkeley, 1965.

TWO-YEAR
STUDENTS
COMPARED
WITH
FOUR-YEAR
STUDENTS

As a group, two-year students, as compared with four-year students, represent a much wider range of ability and achievement, come from homes lower in the socioeconomic scale, are less likely to be motivated for college work, and are more likely to be employed while attending college.

Project Talent studies, including data from a 5 percent sample of some 400,000 high school students who did or did not go on to college, led Cooley and Becker (1966, pp. 464–469) to conclude that junior college students were more like noncollege youth than four-year college students in terms of ability. On all of 14 measures of ability the junior college group fell between four-year students and noncollege groups. In the SCOPE study (Tillery et al., 1966) of 1966 graduates in four states it was found that of students entering universities and colleges 59 percent came from the highest quartile of ability, 26 percent from the second quartile, 11 percent from the third, and about 4 percent from the lowest. The overall figures already reported for the junior college group were 20, 31, 32, and 17 respectively.

Differences between students entering two- and four-year colleges (including universities) and those not entering college at all are portrayed in Charts 7 through 9. The distribution curve for the junior college group approaches the normal on academic aptitude, intellectual predisposition, and family occupational level, whereas the curve for the four-year college group ascends from low to high and the curve for the noncollege students is nearly the reverse.

CHART 7
Distribution of academic aptitude level for students choosing alternative pursuits after high school (1966 SCOPE seniors)

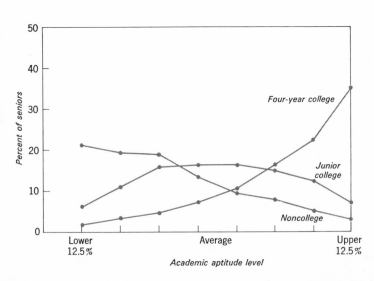

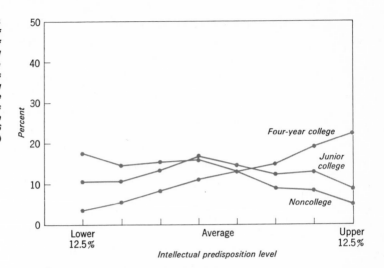

CHART 8
Distribution of levels of intellectual predisposition for students choosing alternative pursuits after high school (1966 SCOPE seniors)

The general resemblance between the noncollege and junior college groups is evident, particularly on the intellectual predisposition scales.

Further evidence of differences in socioeconomic levels of students in two- and four-year colleges is apparent from a synthesis made by Cross (1968). This is illustrated in Table 10. An interesting aspect of these findings is the similarity in socioeconomic background between students entering public two-year colleges and those enrolling in public four-year colleges of nonuniversity

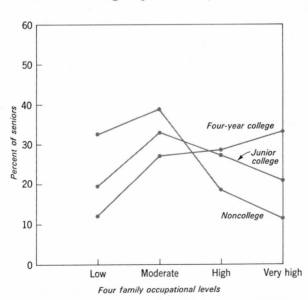

CHART 9
Distribution of family occupational levels for students choosing alternative pursuits after high school (1966 SCOPE seniors)

type. However, public two-year college students, as a group, are from a considerably lower socioeconomic background than are university students. This is not surprising, since various studies have shown that existence of a public two-year college in a community materially increases the number of high school graduates from lower socioeconomic homes who continue their education. In a study authorized by the California Coordinating Council for Higher Education (1967) the investigators concluded that of students in the state's three segments of public higher education, those attending junior colleges demonstrated the greatest financial need.

A variety of factors relate to possible differences in motivation between students in two- and four-year colleges. Data from Astin and his associates (1967) show that junior college freshmen are less confident than four-year college and university freshmen on academic, leadership, mathematical, and writing ability traits as well as on drive to achieve and intellectual self-confidence. The SCOPE data on intellectual predisposition show that a much higher percentage (42.2) of students in universities and colleges came from the highest quartile on the scale than did students in junior colleges (22.7). Medsker and Trent (1965) found that in general junior college students are more conventional, less independent,

TABLE 10
Percentage of students from different socioeconomic backgrounds attending eight types of institutions (in rank order)

Type of institution	Fathers with college*	Fathers with college†	Family over $10,000*	Fathers— professional or managerial†
Private university	64	61	64	49
Private four-year college	63		60	
Catholic four-year college	54	32	54	43
Protestant four-year college	51		51	
Public university	49	49	49	35
Private two-year college	39	39	42	20
Public four-year college	34	31	33	19
Public two-year college	34	29	40	16

*Based on American Council on Education data.
†Based on Medsker-Trent data.

less attracted to reflective thought, and less tolerant than their peers in four-year colleges.

Students in junior college are much more likely to make their final decision on college either late in their high school career or after high school graduation than those who go to four-year colleges. Also as a group junior college students report much less discussion with friends, parents, and others about college than their peers who entered four-year colleges and universities.

There is a great amount of overlap in the characteristics of students at two- and four-year colleges. This overlap illustrated by Medsker (1960) nearly 10 years ago is as evident today as it was then, and it argues against any tendency to generalize that students in four-year colleges are superior to those in two-year colleges.

COLLEGE PARALLEL COMPARED WITH VOCATIONAL-TECHNICAL STUDENTS

To what extent are there differences in the characteristics of students enrolled in college parallel programs compared with those engaged in vocational-technical programs? An answer is difficult because the definition of the two types of programs is ambiguous and the availability of measuring instruments is inadequate. It is hard to distinguish who is actually a "transfer" or a "vocational" student. Whereas about two-thirds of all entering community college students claim they expect to transfer, only one-third actually do. Those who believe they will transfer may or may not be enrolled in courses that carry transfer credit. On the other hand, some courses designed primarily for occupational training are transferable. It has also long been recognized that the conventional types of academic aptitude are not sufficient indicators of important differences among students in unconventional programs at the college level. While students completely oriented to college parallel programs usually score higher than students in vocational-technical programs, this fact does not underscore any real differences. One potential means of overcoming this deficit is the battery of tests known as the Comparative Guidance and Placement Program developed by the Educational Testing Service. The battery has been administered in some 60 comprehensive community colleges and includes tests on reading, vocabulary, verbal ability, sentences, spelling, English, mathematics, inductive reasoning, and perceptual speed and accuracy. Preliminary results show that the college parallel students show the greatest overall mastery of basic skills while those in vocational courses show the least. Technical students fall in between the two groups.

Cross (1969) reports other information about differences in the characteristics of students in the three curricula in 63 of the comprehensive colleges in which the new tests are being administered. In brief, and perhaps not surprisingly, it has been found that students in the college parallel programs come from higher socioeconomic levels than students in either technical or vocational programs. However, students in technical programs come from homes considerably higher in socioeconomic level than do those in less sophisticated vocational programs.

Obviously, more research is needed before meaningful comparisons can be made of students following various curriculum patterns. A comparison of human characteristics itself is not the principal objective; to the extent that differences can be detected and analyzed, a better job of counseling and placement can be done.

ETHNIC GROUPS IN COMMUNITY COLLEGES
To what extent are community colleges drawing from disadvantaged ethnic groups? A review of the community college in the urban setting is found in Chapter 5. There it is reported that special attention to the question of how the community colleges are serving various ethnic groups is widespread. Generally speaking, these colleges attract a higher proportion of disadvantaged students than do other types of institutions, but they still do not draw a representative proportion of the ethnic groups.

CHARACTER-ISTICS OF FUTURE STUDENTS
What are the characteristics of future students likely to be, and to what extent will they enter the community college? There is much speculation about the degree to which attendance at some type of postsecondary school will become universal. Already more than half of the nation's high school graduates continue their education in some type of school or college, and many long out of high school are following suit. With improved access to such education and with a prevailing societal belief that education beyond the high school is important, the proportion can be expected to increase. And since a high percentage of students from upper ability and socioeconomic levels already go to college, it is apparent that the "new" students will be from lower levels on almost any scale used to describe those who attend college.

An insight into the possibilities may be obtained from additional SCOPE data on the 1966 high school graduating class. Of the nearly 20 percent of the seniors who said they planned to go to college but did not, only 12 percent were from the high quartile,

20 percent from the second, 31 percent from the third, and 37 percent from the lowest. Obviously, the students in the last two groups constitute a great pool of potentially new students. Of more than 28 percent of the seniors who said they did not plan to go to college and did not go, only 5.5 percent were from the top group. The percentages in the other quartile groups were 16, 35, and 44 respectively. It is likely that those in the group which to date have said they did not plan to continue their education will contribute significantly to the supply of postsecondary students in the future.

With such trends as the increasing selectivity of four-year colleges, the creation of upper-division colleges, and new emphasis on nonbaccalaureate programs, it can be assumed that the two-year college will inevitably absorb many of the "new" students. Turnbull (1967) expressed this succinctly:

> To look at the student body along the narrow dimensions of academic talent is, of course, grossly inadequate. For the students newly represented in college rolls, skills and aptitudes of quite different orders are probably the pertinent dimensions of comparison. It is symptomatic of our problem that we do not have the data to show systematically the ways in which the college-going population is changing with respect to dimensions other than scholastic aptitude. . . . Clearly, in education we are moving away from the relatively uniform academic program of earlier decades to a much more diversified assortment of offerings. At the higher education level, the community college in particular offers a ready example of an institution that has accepted just this responsibility.

PUBLIC VS. PRIVATE JUNIOR COLLEGE STUDENTS How do students entering public two-year colleges compare with those entering independent junior colleges? Relatively limited data are available which permit such a comparison. Furthermore, it is important that different types of private junior colleges be viewed separately since they vary among themselves in the clientele they serve. Data reported in Table 11 from the four-state SCOPE project suggest that the church-related colleges are more selective in terms of academic ability than either the nondenominational or the public two-year colleges and that the public and nondenominational attract students with similar ability. The differences among the types are fewer with respect to intellectual predisposition except for the much higher percentage of students ranking highest on the scale who attended Catholic colleges. Somewhat surprising is the large proportion of students from high and very high family occupational groups who entered "other religious" colleges and the fact that

TABLE 11 *Distribution by categories of 1966 high school graduates in four states who entered various types of junior colleges, in percents**

Junior college control	Academic ability quartiles				Intellectual predisposition quartiles				Family occupational level			
	Highest	*Above average*	*Below average*	*Lowest*	*Highest*	*Above average*	*Below average*	*Lowest*	*Very high*	*High*	*Moderate*	*Low*
Public	19	30	32	18	24	26	30	21	21	26	34	19
Catholic	47	27	22	4	28	30	28	14	21	29	28	22
Other religion	20	39	33	8	20	30	31	19	25	35	25	16
Nondenominational	18	33	31	16	19	27	31	22	17	28	33	22
TOTAL	20	31	32	17	23	27	30	21	21	27	33	19

*Due to rounding, the figures do not always add to 100.
SOURCE: SCOPE Project, Center for Research and Development in Higher Education, University of California, Berkeley.

fewer students from these high groups entered nondenominational colleges than went to public institutions. It might normally be assumed that high tuition and other costs at most independent colleges would result in a larger proportion of their students' coming from high socioeconomic levels. Conceivably, the SCOPE sample does not allow for the differences that would be found in many high-cost private junior colleges or for emerging differences due to the cost factors discussed in Chapter 8.

Somewhat similar findings regarding the academic ability of public and private junior college students are available from the Medsker-Trent study (1965). It found that of the graduates entering independent junior colleges 25 percent came from the upper ability quintile. This was also true of those entering public two-year colleges. While the independent colleges drew somewhat more heavily from the second quintile ability level than did the public community colleges (29 and 20 percent respectively), they admitted a smaller percentage from the lowest quintile (11 percent of those entering these colleges were from this quintile compared with 17 percent in the public institutions). Another comparison of interest is that the students entering private four-year colleges and universities represented ability levels far higher than those entering the private two-year colleges.

It should be emphasized that the foregoing information about students in independent colleges does not necessarily characterize any one such college nor do the data reported from the SCOPE project imply that students from the sample in the four states entered independent two-year colleges located in those states.

THE OLDER STUDENT Nothing has been said thus far about the "older" community college student—and many are beyond the recent high school age bracket. Some are enrolled full time, taking a regular program in academic or technical-vocational courses, others are doing the same on a part-time basis, and still thousands of others are pursuing a part-time program in conventional adult education courses. A paucity of information exists about most of these older students, particularly the ones attending part-time. That they have jobs and family responsibilities and are highly motivated goes without saying, but information about their various abilities, interests, and intellectual predispositions is still needed. More than any other institution, the community college seems destined to become the most significant medium for continuing education—the educational center in its local community—but it will need data about its clients in order to do its job well.

Student Persistence Still another student characteristic worthy of consideration is that of persistence. The public community college has been criticized for its lack of holding power. The most frequent statistic alluded to is the one shown in Chart 10 which indicates that for public two-year colleges as a group second-year enrollment tends to be less than half of first-year enrollment, thus suggesting more than a 50 percent attrition rate.

Of the more than 22,000 new students who entered, as shown by a sample of community colleges studied in 1961, more than 54 percent withdrew with less than 60 units, and about two-thirds completed no more than one year. However, one-fourth of the group that left transferred to another institution. Doubtless others left to accept employment utilizing skills acquired in the community college.

It is appropriate that concern about the lack of persistence among community college students be expressed. The record would suggest that the colleges themselves are failing to offer programs and services of a nature and in a manner that hold students. This problem should be one of the greatest priorities for research and deliberation on the part of those individuals in state agencies responsible for the planning of community colleges. On the other hand, it is

CHART 10 *Comparison of freshman and sophomore enrollments in public community colleges, 1958–1967.*

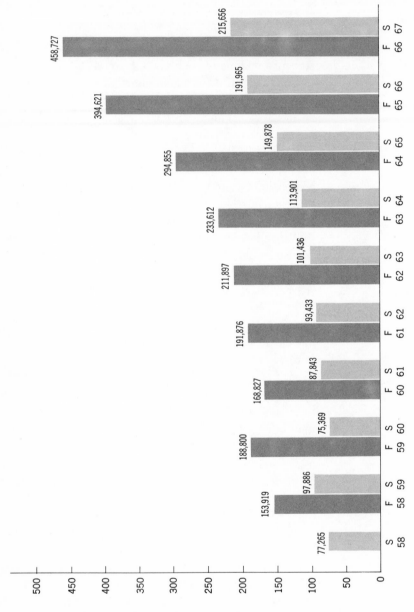

Note that freshman and sophomore data are for consecutive years.

SOURCE: American Association of Junior Colleges.

totally inappropriate to view all student attrition as a "dropout" problem. Many students transfer to a four-year college before completing two years in a community college. Of even greater significance is the fact that students often remain in the community college until they have satisfied some personal or vocational need and then leave to pursue employment or other activities. The fact that they do not remain for two years is not of itself cause for criticism, especially if the community college is viewed as a flexible institution capable of serving various types of needs.

CONCLUSIONS The data presented in this chapter document many generalizations. Junior college students, particularly those in public community colleges, are diverse. They come from many backgrounds, have varying personal endowments, and seek to fulfill many purposes.

This results naturally from the established policy of community colleges that any high school graduate can be admitted. In most of the states, legislation provides that older youth and adults who have not completed high school may also be admitted. Currently there is widespread discussion about the principle of open enrollment in all institutions of higher education. Colleges as well as state governing boards throughout the country are grappling with the question of how far they should go in applying the concept. It may be that it will be applied more within the total system of postsecondary education in each of the states than in all individual institutions. In this case, the community colleges will play an increasingly important role in providing opportunity for all who wish to continue their education. This, in turn, will accentuate the diversity of their student bodies. Thus, while the "new students" are already in community colleges, greater numbers of them will be admitted in the future, and this will effect a new mix of students. This naturally has implications for the curriculum, instruction, student personnel services, physical facilities, and a host of other matters with which the community college must be concerned.

4. A Program for All

There is a growing consensus about the nature of the program of the comprehensive community college, which can best be summed up as a program for all. True, some students, governmental officials, and educational leaders continue to be concerned about the gap between what these colleges promise to do and what they are able to achieve. Nevertheless, this uniquely American institution has proved its great worth to society and is having a profound impact on higher education here, while challenging educators from a score of other nations. Understanding the objectives of the comprehensive program is essential if one is to understand the claims and criticisms of the community college.

The program, designed to serve the most diverse population of youth and adults in all of education, encompasses six main functions—preparation for advanced study, career education, guidance, developmental education, general education, and community service. While recognizing these several functions, the Executive Director of the American Association of Junior Colleges stresses the institution's responsibility to provide learning experiences which other colleges cannot or will not provide and to serve students whom others cannot or will not serve (Gleazer, 1968). However, an aggregate of courses and services cannot meet these expectations which Gleazer and other leaders have for the community colleges, nor does a description of the program components tell the story.

The comprehensive program of the two-year colleges is more than the sum of its parts. It must be rationally planned, coordinated, and renewed so that students are enabled through classroom and guidance experiences to reexamine their educational and career goals and to change directions if they so choose.

The educational package designed for each student from the

several components of the comprehensive program is what makes the community college something special. It may be that the story of how these pieces fit together can only be told through the lives of students. Before discussing the issues related to the several functions of the comprehensive program, it may be helpful to sketch briefly the ways in which several students have been served by the scope and interrelatedness of what goes on in the colleges they attended. The following vignettes are based on the lives of real students. John, Sarah, Bill, and Joan are *not* typical students because there are no typical students. They are, however, successful students, and the brief accounts of their college experiences illustrate ways in which the several functions of the community college program fit together.

John, the frustrated fireman, first learned about his community college while attending an industrial safety conference conducted by the college's community service program. The conference team encouraged him to try an introductory chemistry course he regretted missing in high school. John did just that and hit it off well with his chemistry instructor, who liked the young fireman's maturity and diligence. He was baffled, however, by John's modest high school record.

On the advice of a counselor with whom the teacher discussed his concerns, the latter suggested to John that he might want to take some aptitude and interest tests. John did, and for several weeks the three—student, teacher, and counselor—worked together as John sought to know himself better. First, he was amazed to learn that he had very high scores on tests related to scientific interests and aptitudes. Later, he discovered that there were ways of developing and expressing these capacities without sacrificing his years of experience and his interest in fire prevention.

John had a number of tough decisions to make and much hard work ahead, because he finally decided to prepare at the state university for advanced studies in scientific fire prevention. For some time he used the day and evening programs of the community college while continuing his work as fireman. Later, on leave from the department, he transferred to the state university and completed a Master of Science program. Among the contributions he made to fire prevention after returning to his home town was the development, in cooperation with his community college counselor, of a program for selecting and training new firemen. John also was appointed to the college's advisory committee for its own fire-training program.

Sarah, the potential teacher, was outwardly unresponsive to teachers and fellow students when she took her first night course at the local community college. She dealt with unhappiness at home by cooking for her foster family and by stuffing herself to the point of obesity. But she also read extensively, and this spark was carefully fanned by her college instructor. Nevertheless, Sarah was hostile to suggestions that she might want to explore a major in literature.

Sarah reluctantly began educational counseling, but soon revealed her fears of losing the precarious place she held in her adopted family if she should give any serious attention to her own education and career aspirations. Her expressed interest in teaching was readily supported by aptitude and interest testing, but to Sarah it was to be a compromise all the way. Since preparing for being a teacher at the nearby state college might break the bond with her family, she chose a part-time program which would prepare her to become a teacher's aide. The program was one of a group of paraprofessional programs which the college offered for youth and adults preparing for careers, usually after two years of study.

For some readers, Sarah's will not be seen as a success story, but to her it still is. She found new confidence in herself, new talents, and new strength in working toward her own independence. Upon completion of her Associate in Arts degree, she hesitantly accepted a position as a teaching aide in a state school for the blind. Sarah found that she not only acquired increasing skill in teaching her blind students, but that she could give and accept love from them. Those who worked with her continued to encourage Sarah to complete work toward a teaching credential. She responded by continuing night courses at her community college, but saying how difficult it would be to leave her "new family."

Bill, the enlightened electrician, was well into the second semester of a two-year program to prepare electricians when he and his instructor discovered something about him which greatly changed his life. Bill had been in the Navy for several years and said that it took some courage, as a black man with three children, to abandon his work as a naval electrician to return to school. His choice of a program in electricity seemed appropriate, but he soon discovered that he was more interested in the mathematics and theory than in the practical work of his courses. These interests led to friendly and lengthy discussions with his teacher which began to challenge both of them. Was Bill in the right program after all? Why not try the next course in mathemetics and maybe a course in physics? A number of people, including science and math instructors and members of the guidance staff, helped find answers to these and related questions.

The evidence began to mount: Bill had clearly underestimated his abilities and his motivation. Even after the second semester had begun, it was agreed that he should shift gears and prepare for electrical engineering. The program changes were easily made, although some special tutorial work was necessary to compensate him for inadequacies in his early school preparation.

Bill did well in his new program and soon began a series of visits to state colleges to explore with his counselor how best to prepare for advanced study. He soon transferred to a state college without loss of credit and earned his Bachelor of Science degree on schedule. He and his supporters at the community college recognized how important the GI Bill had been in his career transformation. By devoting himself full-time to his studies, he had been able to take advantage of the instruction, guidance, and tutorial assistance offered by the college.

Joan, the competitive coed, was near the top of her high school graduating class. Both she and her parents had for years assumed she would go to college, and many of her teachers had encouraged her to think seriously about going to graduate school. As a matter of fact, her school counselor had arranged several visits to college campuses, including one to a distinguished private liberal arts college some distance from her home. None of those who advised Joan had considered the local community college appropriate for her.

In early spring, Joan's father became seriously ill and her mother decided to quit her job as a department store buyer so that she might take care of him. Even though Joan had received a state scholarship, she became painfully aware of the financial crisis at home and its implication for her college plans.

"Why not go to city college for your first two years and then transfer to a senior college which has a good sociology department?" asked her boyfriend, who had already decided to attend the local college. The question disturbed Joan.

"Won't I lose some credits upon transferring?" she asked. "Will I have enough competition in my classes to make them stimulating? Isn't the community college for kids who are preparing for jobs?" She consulted the community college counselor who visited her high school that spring. Later she visited the campus and, to her surprise, found it not at all like high school. She was very impressed with the teachers she met and by the discovery that students learned at their own pace.

Joan decided to live at home, defer use of her state scholarship, and seek a part-time job at the local college. The fall quarter was rewarding: she worked as a tutor in an inner-city project and found her relationships with her teachers friendly and intellectually stimulating. She even began to think of teaching in a community college.

Even though Joan could have transferred following her father's recovery, she decided to stay at city college until she received her Associate in Arts degree. Then, with money in the bank and a new sense of independence, she transferred to the private college she had dreamed of for so long. As predicted, she was admitted to junior standing and found herself well prepared to compete with advanced students who had originally entered the college from high school.

These four students were served in individual ways by teachers and counselors, working with comprehensive programs, who knew how to interrelate the several parts in the educational and career development of students. When there are serious shortcomings in college programs or in the skill and commitment of faculty, students who might otherwise develop their full potential in the open-door colleges may not experience anything like these four "success" stories. In the following discussion of the several functions of the comprehensive program, attention will be given to both the opportunities and problems involved.

PREPARATION FOR ADVANCED STUDY The first junior colleges were established to provide interim education for those who could not enter senior colleges immediately after high school. This early trickle of students who had academic, financial, or personal reasons for deferring entry into traditional colleges and universities has grown into a flood of young men and women who channel themselves into junior colleges and then into a wide range of senior institutions. Nationally, at least one-third of all high school graduates who enter college choose this route, while in Florida and California this is true of 69 and 80 percent, respectively, of entering college students.

This staggering educational responsibility is complicated by the fact that only a minority of junior college students are eligible to enter most senior colleges at the time of high school graduation. Nevertheless, repeated studies show that over two-thirds of entering students *plan* to transfer to senior colleges or universities. Regardless of the number who actually transfer, extensive pretransfer programs must be offered. In 1968, for example, 1.4 million students were enrolled in pretransfer programs. Central to the concept of the comprehensive community college is the opportunity, through guidance and program exploration, for students to change educational and career directions. Such redirection of pretransfer students is only partially successful, and some drop out of college with little preparation for gainful employment. About one-third of the entering junior college freshmen do, in fact, transfer, and a majority of these earn a baccalaureate degree (Medsker and Trent, 1965).

Articulation of Junior and Senior Colleges Although articulation between junior and senior colleges is improving under the influence of state master plans and central coordination, the effectiveness of the two-year-college programs may be limited by traditional curricula in the senior institutions. Perhaps the problems imposed by transfer requirements of state universities, in particular, are more imagined than real. It is more likely that many junior college faculty leaders share the educational conservatism of their senior college colleagues (Medsker, 1960). Whatever the cause, the transfer programs of numerous junior colleges are too closely modeled after those of the state universities to fit the needs of many students with the potential for advanced study but with educational deficiencies from high school.

In an increasing number of states the majority of lower-division students are enrolled in the public community colleges. It seems inevitable that the faculties of these colleges will play more significant roles in determining the curriculum for the first two years. Their struggle to do so will not be easy, although current student discontent may make this a most propitious time to seek new accommodations between the faculties of two- and four-year institutions.

How well students from junior colleges achieve after transferring to four-year colleges remains a matter of interest to educators and policy makers. Although continuing studies are needed, especially in states with little tradition in the movement of students from two- to four-year institutions, the evidence points to academic success for most transfer students. Those junior college transfer students who were fully eligible to enter senior college at the time of high school graduation do very well. A majority of transfer students earned their eligibility for admission to senior college while in junior colleges. Some of these have difficulty in persisting, but those who do improve after the first semester following transfer.

Knoell and Medsker (1964, p. 178) studied students in 10 states who transferred from two- to four-year institutions and reported that "The cumulative average at the four-year college for the entire group (of transfer students) was found to be 2.34, or C+, compared with a cumulative junior college average of 2.56."

Although recent studies have indicated steady improvement in the ease with which students transfer from two- to four-year colleges, there is a need in many states for more careful articulation of policies providing for transfer (Willingham, 1969). Neither the program of the junior college nor its students should be subject to vagaries in admission policies of senior institutions. It is important that whenever public four-year institutions are forced, because of inadequacies of budgets, to turn away students who meet their admission requirements, top priority should be given to qualified students transferring from community colleges. Private colleges and universities should also develop policies encouraging the admission of community college graduates.

Virtually all faculty members in community colleges consider preparation for transfer to be an essential function of their institutions. Many educators believe that teachers emphasize this function to the detriment of other aspects of the program. Nevertheless, an increasing proportion of undergraduates enrolled in degree credit programs will be in two-year colleges. In view of the large proportion of students enrolled in transfer programs, major emphasis on improving the quality of these programs will continue to be required (Carnegie Commission, June, 1970, p. 18).

CAREER EDUCATION Americans are highly pragmatic about education, and most students describe the goals of their education as essentially occupational (Tillery et al., 1969). Nevertheless, a minority of two-year college students declare vocational majors upon entering college.

The resistance to occupational programs by many students who might profit from them has long disturbed community college leaders. This resistance has been mitigated somewhat by the development of well-taught and excellently equipped programs in 30 to 50 occupational curricula. These include programs in science, electronic and engineering technologies, paramedical fields, health, government, and recreation services, skilled trades and crafts, agriculture, horticulture, forestry, business, commerce, and the applied and graphic arts.

Community college leaders have worked diligently to define a level of occupational education which would differentiate such preparation for employment from secondary occupational programs and from those of special postsecondary schools. In spite of warnings (Harris, 1964 and Venn, 1964), some colleges may have set too high standards for some of their occupational curricula. The carefully developed technical and semiprofessional programs of the community colleges frequently have such high standards that they must compete for students who aspire to transfer to senior colleges. Neglect of appropriate employment preparation for many students of modest ability and achievement seriously limits the comprehensiveness of the community college program. The open door promises what it sometimes fails to offer. While community colleges have been wise in developing programs which have clearly earned the respect of employers, nevertheless, there is great urgency for these colleges to enter a new phase of cooperation with business, industry, and government to train and retrain youth and adults who have been educationally neglected.

Whereas the past decade has seen spectacular development in training for paramedical occupations and for electronic and engineering technology, the community colleges now are beginning to offer programs, at several levels of leadership and specialized skills, in service occupations. Few institutions are so well prepared to meet these needs or have so many students with appropriate interests and talents. The development of such new programs will follow only if faculties are convinced that human talents are far more varied than those traditionally valued.

The attitudes of faculties to certain components of occupational education may be related to the pecking order within occupational programs and between academic and occupational education. Whereas there is widespread belief among community college teachers that education should be provided for those students who

| | Faculty attitudes in percent | | |
Program	Essential	Optional	Inappropriate
Technical or semiprofessional two-year program	85	14	1
Preemployment curricula for skilled and semiskilled employment	50	37	11
Preemployment or in-service training for adults	34	54	12
Retraining of technologically unemployed adults	27	54	18
Short-term occupational programs	21	49	26

TABLE 12 *Faculty attitudes toward aspects of occupational education*

Approximately 1 percent nonresponses not shown.
SOURCE: Medsker, unpublished data from study of 57 junior colleges, 1967.

seek job preparation as well as for those who wish to transfer, there is little agreement on the importance of the several components which are common elements of the comprehensive program.

Very few faculty members perceive technical and vocational education as inappropriate (Table 12), although only the first is seen as essential by most respondents. Only half of the faculty members believe preemployment curricula for skilled and semiskilled employment to be essential in their colleges, and a small minority feel strongly about the importance of short-term occupational courses and programs to retrain technically unemployed adults. Nevertheless, Table 12 clearly shows that only a minority of teachers actually reject any of these components as inappropriate. A basis for constructive responses to increasing social pressures on the community colleges to provide education for youth and adults not served by other segments of higher education is apparent in these data. But the essential faculty commitment is by no means universal. It seems evident that community colleges still invite through their open doors students for whom no appropriate educational programs exist—and whom some teachers do not welcome.

Using data from nearly a decade ago, Venn (1964, p. 88) concluded that "Taken as a whole, American junior colleges do not give proper attention to the occupational phase of their purpose." At that time less than a quarter of all junior college students in the United States were enrolled in organized occupational curricula. One-third of California's junior college students were in occupational curricula, but other states with considerable junior college development had only token enrollments in such programs.

State	Transfer programs	Occupational programs	Total	Percent occupational
California	399,999	200,831	600,830	33
Florida	76,443	18,976	95,419	20
Illinois	82,929	30,787	113,716	27
Michigan	65,955	33,763	99,718	34
Texas	77,823	19,177	97,000	20
Washington	42,135	24,670	66,805	37
Aggregate United States	1,293,487	502,939	1,796,426	28

New York, one of the pacesetter states, is not included because it classifies most enrollments as degree-credit. This practice results in an underestimate of occupational enrollments in the aggregate United States.
SOURCE: Adapted from U.S. Office of Education, National Center for Educational Statistics, 1968, pp. 12–13.

During the 1960s there was an increase in the proportion of students enrolled in occupational programs—from about one-quarter to at least one-third. It is difficult to determine the current ratio because of the practice in some states, such as New York, to classify nearly all enrollments as degree-credit.

Table 13 suggests that California junior colleges have stabilized, with one-third of their students in formal preparation for employment. The state of Washington, on the other hand, has not only made dramatic gains in community college development, but has given special attention to occupational education. Washington tops the pacesetters with 37 percent of its two-year college students in curricula which prepare them for employment.

In its recent special report (June, 1970, p. 21) the Carnegie Commission on Higher Education recommends "coordinated efforts at the federal, state, and local levels to stimulate the expansion of occupational education in community colleges and to make it responsive to changing manpower requirements. Continuing education for adults, as well as occupational education for college-age students, should be provided." The promises of the community colleges are now being taken seriously by a new generation of students and by government alike. To fulfill them, a few innovations in program will not be enough; new commitment and new approaches to career education will be demanded.

GUIDANCE   Guidance has a central role in the community colleges. This unique orientation for an institution of higher education results in part from widespread faculty convictions (McConnell, 1967, p. ii, Preface) that

. . . if students are to choose wisely among different courses and curricula leading to a great variety of future careers, they must be assisted in identifying their abilities and aptitudes, in assessing their deficiencies and their potentialities, and in rationalizing their aspirations.

There is also general recognition that the early college years are important in the self-identity of youth. Since many community college students have not developed clear educational and vocational goals and are unusually vulnerable to interrelated financial, academic, and personal pressures, their guidance needs are particularly crucial. This means that guidance is everybody's business and not just that of the professional counselors.

In a sense, community colleges are distribution centers where important educational and career decisions are made before students move on to immediate employment or to senior colleges. But for every student who moves from junior to senior college, there are two who move directly into the world of work. For some, these outcomes seem to be educational short circuits, while for others they are the outcome of redirection through effective counseling. A recommendation of the Carnegie Commission on Higher Education (June, 1970, *ibid.,* pp. 21–22) seems essential if the distribution function of the community college is to be effective.

It is particularly important for all students to recognize that, whether they choose a transfer, general education, or occupational program, the ultimate objective is preparation for an occupation. Increasingly, in fact, the prevailing pattern is for married women to return to the labor force once their children are all in school. Thus, a primary objective of guidance programs should be to encourage students to make wise choices between curricula that are specifically designed to prepare for an occupation and those that are designed to lead to ultimate career choices that benefit from more prolonged academic education preceding specialization. If students can be led to understand these distinctions clearly, the tendency to regard occupational curricula as "dead-end" or inferior may be overcome.

The Commission recommends that all community colleges should provide adequate resources for effective guidance, including not only provision for an adequate professional counseling staff, but also provision for involvement of the entire faculty in guidance of students enrolled in their courses. The Commission also recommends that all community college districts provide for effective coordination of their guidance services with those of local high schools and for coordination of both counseling and place-ment services with those of the public employment offices and other appro-priate agencies.

Medsker's recent study of junior colleges shows that two-thirds of the faculty members recognize guidance as an integral part of the educational program in their colleges. Guidance services are provided both by professional counselors and by members of the faculty. Nevertheless, during the past decade there appears to have been only modest improvement in planning for guidance services and in their organization and management. Although unsupported by systematic evidence, there is widespread belief that many com-munity colleges are reorganizing their guidance services to bring counselors into physical proximity to the teaching faculties, and, hopefully, into better communication with peers and students. New programs for the preparation of counselors stress their role in working with faculty as well as face to face with students.

College counselors' concerns for the dynamics of educational and career problems of their clients have often led to misunder-standings with teachers and administrators. Both groups complain about the psychological or therapeutic orientation of counselors as well as their apparent lack of interest and experience in the world of work. The counselors, in turn, have been burdened by counselor-student ratios which should embarrass any community college advocate. The Carnegie study of guidance in two-year colleges showed that the recommended ratio of 1 to 300 is only achieved exceptionally (Raines, 1966).

It is likely that soon there will be as many adult students in junior colleges as there are youth immediately out of high school. The implications of this for guidance programs are profound, since only a few junior colleges now have older students, and many do not even have regular counseling services available for the thousands of adults in evening divisions. Collins (1970) notes that "older students returning to school after many years of absence have fears, aspirations and attitudes different from those of the recent high school graduate; they doubtless require a kind of orientation different from the stock 'ease-them-out-of-puberty' introduction to college."

An important new possibility for community college guidance ser-vices is to move them off the campus. Storefront guidance centers have been helpful in motivating alienated youth and adults. Cooperative guidance services with feeder high schools are improving the articulation of secondary programs with those of the local college. However, these new services are all too rare, and it is clear that recruiting new students is not yet part of the main thrust.

Guidance will assume increasing importance as the community colleges continue to emphasize the educability of all students, the exploration of opportunities, and the development of individual interests and talents.

DEVELOP-MENTAL EDUCATION Efforts to remedy learning deficiencies cut across all segments of the comprehensive program of the community college. It is estimated that 30 to 50 percent of students enter the open-door colleges in need of the basic skills required for college study. This is as true for those who aspire to advanced education as it is for those who seek preparation for employment. Some colleges have huge numbers of students who are seriously in need of remediation, while others have manageable numbers who need to improve their reading, writing, and mathematical skills. As barriers to educational opportunity are eliminated, students in need of help will "flood the community colleges and greatly exacerbate the present problems of providing developmental and remedial training . . ." (Collins and Collins, 1966).

The components of the developmental function are as follows:

Developmental reading is taught increasingly by trained reading specialists in properly equipped laboratories. There is little doubt that well-conducted reading programs are bringing many students up to reasonable standards in reading speed, comprehension, and vocabulary. Nevertheless, there still is a shortage of instructional materials which are properly graduated and which are stimulating to students who have few traditional academic interests.

Remedial composition probably accounts for greater effort on the part of college faculties—and more student suffering—than other aspects of the program. Even students with reading and mathematical competence may not be able to write. Increasingly, writing and spelling drill is being replaced by instruction to help students understand the nature and power of language. Transcriptions of oral reports, particularly for students of ethnic backgrounds, are being used for joint editing by students and tutors. Nevertheless, the standard yardstick for measuring student success is still the traditional freshman course in English composition. For many students, standards more relevant to occupations are needed.

Remedial programs in mathematics are increasingly important. Some students must renew basic arithmetic skills, while others must take, for the first time, beginning courses in the mathematics sequence which have been shifted in recent years to the high school level. "Illiteracy" in mathematics is seen as a threat to survival. Consequently, most community colleges require some achievement in mathematics as part of their general education requirements.

Learning skills have traditionally been considered a by-product of other aspects of remedial education. It is only recently that help for students who simply do not know how to learn has been viewed as an essential component of remediation. Although routine courses in study habits are still common, many are being augmented by applied study of the psychology of motivation and learning.

Developmental speech courses are an increasingly popular and useful experience for community college students. Without the constraints which writing imposes on many people, oral communication can help students to organize their own thoughts and to understand and evaluate the views of others.

The student who is seriously handicapped in one of these basic skills often has difficulty in the others. Consequently, community colleges frequently develop core programs—sometimes euphemistically called opportunity programs—to concentrate efforts to bring handicapped students to reasonable proficiency in a reasonably short time. For some students, these concentrated programs have *not* provided opportunities for learning because they have tended to isolate low-achieving students from courses which really interest them and from students and faculty who might "turn them on." Generally, these core programs leave much to be desired. There is increasing awareness that the developmental function is everybody's business, not just that of the reading or speech therapist and certainly not just that of the hard-pressed English teacher.

In spite of the high percentage of students who need remedial courses, only half of their teachers consider such courses essential to the college program. Medsker's unpublished study (1967) of 57 junior colleges further shows that nearly one-fifth of the faculties believe that such courses actually are inappropriate. It may be that these attitudes help explain the continuation of practices in two-year colleges which seem so inconsistent with the needs of many of the new students. A few of these practices seem particularly central to the problems of educating the undereducated.

Grading. Students are still thrown into destructive competition with one another, and the progress of "remedial" students is frequently measured against standards of courses for which they may not be seeking admission. It should be noted that a number of colleges are experimenting with "nonpunitive grading" systems which eliminate failing grades for those who are trying to learn. When it is apparent that a student can't make it, he is permitted to withdraw from a class without penalty.

Probation. Many students see probation as another brand of failure (the story of their previous schooling) rather than as a means of mobilizing the college's resources to help. Guidance leaders often agree with this assessment of traditional probation policies. There are many efforts among the colleges to modify these policies, including one experiment to abandon probation entirely.

Dismissal. Getting rid of students is not a way to educate them. Dismissing students because they cannot compete well with those who are brighter and better prepared may be acceptable at selective colleges and universities: It is not the mission of the community colleges. This conviction is not fully shared by either faculty, administrators, or trustees of these institutions.

Remedial courses. Traditional remedial courses in the so-called basic skills depress teachers and students alike. They frequently ignore issues of motivation and the individual nature of learning problems. Nevertheless, the successes and failures of these massive efforts of remediation in the community colleges provide the basis for more effective programs, including tutorials, use of new learning techniques, and efforts to stimulate faith in ability to learn.

In a recent study of programs for poorly prepared students, Cross (1970) found that 80 percent of public community colleges have special provisions for students who do not meet the traditional academic requirements for college. Of those colleges, 92 percent offer developmental courses to upgrade verbal and other academic skills, although only 61 percent have special counseling programs for remedial students. It is interesting to note the different practices among the colleges in awarding credit for remedial work:

25 percent offer none; 29 percent give non-degree credit; and 32 percent give degree credits.

There appears to be more concern about and more experimentation with development education than with any other component of the community college program. The new uses of learning technologies and individual tutorials are both promising and costly. It seems imperative that additional resources be brought to the efforts of reeducation. This will happen only if there is widespread conviction that such efforts are important if the community colleges are to fulfill their mission.

GENERAL EDUCATION Learning experiences which convey the interrelationships of human knowledge, which invite the student to perceive, appreciate, and respond to the diversity and beauty of the world and humanity about him have been the broad goals of general education. It is more specifically defined in the following statement of Diablo Valley Junior College (1969–70, p. 20), which is typical of those found in community college catalogs:

> Diablo Valley College encourages all students to have a body of common course experiences, the results of which are known as general education. The ultimate aim of general education is the "educated man" in its broadest sense. This is man possessed of understanding and information about our culture both past and present. This is man able to operate as a rational human being in our society.
>
> The faculty believes that the subject matter of general education should be presented in a way which shows how one piece of knowledge and life is related to many others — an integrated approach to teaching and learning. It believes the subject matter must be presented in a manner which will encourage the student to develop and evaluate values in terms of man's relationship to and with himself, to and with others, and to and with his environment. It further believes that this subject matter and these goals require a rigorous involvement in the content of the various academic disciplines and that this approach is appropriate for all students at this college.
>
> While most courses contribute in some way to general education, certain courses have been identified as ones in which conscious attention is given to this important aspect of education.

This catalog, like those of most other community colleges, lists a pattern of courses which must be taken to meet the general education requirements for the Associate in Arts degree. Typically, this means about 25 to 30 semester units (about one-third of the units required for the degree) of work in major fields of knowledge — social sciences, humanities, natural sciences; and additional courses in basic skills and in health and physical education.

In spite of the attention faculties give to the *pieces* of enlightenment and their persistent efforts to achieve general education goals, many community college leaders are dissatisfied with the way this aspect of the comprehensive program is being carried out. There are, to be sure, some islands of innovation, but they frequently are submerged by the sea of specialization. Two factors may help explain the frustrations and apparent inadequacies associated with general education programs, namely, the incongruence of means and ends and the failure to evaluate adequately the impact of different approaches on student development.

Mayhew and Dressel, in their study of general education, (1954, p. 272) concluded: "Teachers do commonly admit that it is not possible to determine what knowledge students should possess. . . . None [of the course patterns] possess a logic which can be accepted as valid by all teachers and by all students. . . ." These researchers agreed that "emphasis on and selection of a body of common knowledge is not an adequate basis for further progress in general education." Nevertheless, this is the most common approach in American colleges. In view of the modest efforts to evaluate programs of general education, faith rather than evidence supports continuing efforts in the community colleges, and this faith is by no means universal.

The Problem of Relevance To many students from ethnic minority groups, traditional general education programs based on a body of "common knowledge" are irrelevant, if not outright racist. To the students and faculty who seek to understand *all* mankind, these programs seem strongly ethnocentric in their emphasis upon Western civilization and science. To many in the nonacademic world, the separation of culture and vocation is anathema. Alternatives to such programs have strong roots in the junior college but are not commonly reflected in the curriculum (Johnson, 1952). Feldman (1969, p. 24) believes that "the current tendency to give a student initial general education and then specialization is inappropriate on pedagogical grounds and is at the roots of the major problem in community college education. . . . The intertwining of liberal and vocational elements in an educational program seeking to expand opportunity for a major proportion of our population is both necessary and possible."

In pointing out that general education in the junior college is a culmination of a curriculum that began in elementary school and continued through high school, Reynolds (1969, p. 29) advises program developers to "consider the years preceding junior college for clues as to what the junior college should be, or in order to suggest needed changes in the high school programs." Without such articulation with the secondary schools, general education requirements may become increasingly repetitive and irrelevant.

Mayhew and Dressel (1954, p. 268) pointed out that "the general education movement at its incept derived its energy from the fact that it was a protest movement. . . ." Among the practices in American education to which this protest has been directed are: compartmentalization of knowledge; proliferation of courses; evils of the elective system; content instead of student orientation; and disproportionate emphasis on research. They conclude that "the movement is presently in need of a more positive dynamic—a positive integrating principle to replace the principle of protest." Among the influences for change is the lowering of barriers which separate the major fields of knowledge. The "disciplines" were essentially functional arrangements for research and scholarship, but they never made much sense in structuring the undergraduate curriculum. Now that research has jumped the boundaries of departments, new respectability should accrue to interdisciplinary programs of general education. Because they teach such a large share of undergraduates, it seems quite appropriate for community college faculties to lead in finding new ways to fit the pieces of human knowledge together, helping man to discover who he is and how he can help build a social order that fits him. The two-year colleges have many creative and well-qualified teachers who are ready to accept this challenge. Higher education can profit from their new approaches to general education.

COMMUNITY SERVICE The newest, but inevitable, function of community colleges is that of community service. One of the most informed writers on this function (Harlacher, 1969, p. 5) has challenged the community colleges to:

1 Become a center of community life by encouraging the use of college facilities and services by community groups when such does not interfere with the college's regularly scheduled programs.

2 Provide for all age groups educational services that utilize the special skills and knowledge of the college staff and other experts . . . designed to meet the needs of community groups and the college district community at large.

3 Provide the community, including business and industry, with the leadership and coordination capabilities of the college, assist the community in long-range planning, and join with individuals and groups in attacking unsolved problems.

4 Contribute to and promote the cultural, intellectual, and social life of the college district community and the development of skills for the profitable use of leisure time.

At present, community service is still an emerging function. The rhetoric outstrips the scope of local programs. Harlacher (*ibid.,* p. 42) believes:

One reason for the slow emergence of community services . . . is that many presidents, deans, other administrators, and faculty frequently regard the program of community services as secondary, an amplification of the standard functions, not as a separate function.

He identifies a number of major problem areas which require new staff commitments and leadership for their solutions. These include problems of communication, internally and externally; need for staff and trustee support; coordination of services with those of other local and regional groups; identification of community needs and interests; systematic planning and evaluation; administration and program supervision; financial needs; and finally, the development of a program philosophy and identification of objectives. Harlacher joins many junior college leaders in believing that the great new thrust of the community colleges is toward community service.

The Community College as Home Base Schools and colleges have long been places for the acculturation and renewal of America's citizens—first for millions of immigrants, and more recently for migrants from rural to urban America. Until the development of community colleges, the adult education programs of high schools and the extension programs of the land-grant colleges carried these staggering burdens.

In spite of its continued use, the terminal education concept is increasingly rejected and is in conflict with the present—let alone the future—uses of education in America. The changing nature of the occupational world gives new meaning to continuing education. The widespread conviction is that "the average youth of today will probably shift occupations some five times over the next forty years he is in the labor market. A life of continuing occupational adjustment will mean a life of continuing education to meet changed or additional educational requirements" (Venn, 1964, p. 26). This assessment may already be outdated because our productivity may soon make it unnecessary for any American to stay in the labor market for anything like 40 years. Instead, his return to education may be increasingly for personal and cultural development. In either case, it is likely that the public community colleges will play a prominent, but by no means exclusive, role in such occupational and personal renewal.

Continuing education has rather shallow meaning if the programs for transfer and occupational students alike do not stimulate interest in lifelong development and provide the learning techniques to make it possible. While there is much rhetoric about lifelong education and the relevance of the community college curriculum, most continuing education programs rely heavily on traditional introductory courses or on what many teachers considered to be "watered-down" versions of "college-level" courses. Studies of the backgrounds of many students in two-year colleges suggest that such traditional fare will not do (Tillery, 1964).

The college as a catalyst for self-improvement and as a locus for the cultural, intellectual, and social development of the community is part of the new look for public junior colleges (Harlacher, 1969). The "college for the community" is a phenomenon of this decade, although it grows from the early junior college commitment to respond to community needs.

A brief compendium of services now offered by many community colleges suggests that they are beginning to redeem the promissory notes issued a quarter of a century ago by junior college spokesmen (Gleazer, 1968, p. 86):

Commonly included are educational workshops, seminars; institutes and special lectures; community research and development; wide-spread use of college facilities by community groups; varied cultural programs; community guidance and counseling; cooperation with employers and placement agencies; the utilization of the physical and human resources of the community in the instructional programs of the college; public reformation; and many more.

CONCLUSION   If the comprehensive program is not yet a program for all, many community colleges are striving to make it so. This conviction is widely shared and is reflected in a closing statement on goals of the open-door colleges by the Carnegie Commission on Higher Education (June, 1970, p. 51):

> The community college movement is full of promise for the opportunities it offers to young persons and adults to increase their occupational skills, to get started in an academic career, to enrich the quality of their lives, and generally to multiply their educational options and their chances to choose wisely among them. It offers these opportunities to more Americans in more areas and of more ages than any other segment of higher education.

5. The Junior College and Urban Life

Education which will serve the needs of urban society has given community college development new urgency. Federal legislation which would provide resources and leadership to make community colleges the "best equipped for the job of extending and expanding much-needed educational opportunities in our country" (Williams, 1969) is pending. But as community colleges are pushed onto center stage or, as some would say, seek star billing, they may disrupt emerging efforts to bring all education into the struggle to serve individuals and groups in the cities. Community college leaders are aware of the dangers of "going it alone" and urge faculty and administrators to coordinate their programs and services with other institutions of both secondary and higher education (Cosand, 1969).

Some people call for a new type of higher institution of education which would aggressively attack the problems of the cities in America. While clearly urging the massive development of community colleges in the coming decade, Clark Kerr (1968, p. 6) sees the need for an additional institution:

Many institutions around the country called urban universities have turned their backs on their own cities. I use the term "urban grant" instead, to indicate a type of university which would have an aggressive approach to the problems of the city, where the city itself and its problems would become the animating focus. . . .

Few, however, envision this new "urban university" as a substitute for the community college. Existing and new institutions will need to band together in consortia of schools, colleges, and universities which seek, through coordination of diverse programs, faculties, and resources, to contribute more effectively to the solution of human and environmental problems. A few such consortia are in the early stages of development. Those in San Francisco, St. Louis, Washington, D.C., and Cleveland may help shape the new look of the urban community college.

Community college leaders and federal officials envision the community college as a critical link in an integrated four-stage public system for the nation (Feldman, 1969, pp. 9, 15):

The Community College, the capstone of such a system, would be a transitional institution of higher education. . . . It would be a prime source of education for careers, of academic development, and of personal enrichment for a significant part of the American people and thus a prime contributor to the paramount national goal of enhanced quality of life for all citizens.

To better understand the potential of the community colleges which are now within commuting distance of 82 percent of the 18- to 24-year-old population of major metropolitan areas, it is important to appraise their current response to urban needs.

THE EDUCATION OF MINORITY STUDENTS In his assessment of relevance in postsecondary education, Willingham (1969) concludes that it is not possible to say definitely whether the college access rate of black persons is catching up with the majority or not. However, if one defines minority to include Spanish-speaking Americans and American Indians, it is clear that neither higher education generally nor any segment specifically is providing equal opportunity for minority students. Tillery, within the context of related research, draws this conclusion in interpreting

TABLE 14 Racial composition of enrollments in public junior colleges

Race	SCOPE* 1967	Creager† 1968	CGP‡ 1969
Caucasian	84	84	84
Negro	8	9	8
Oriental	2	2	3
Other	6	5	(5)

*SOURCE: Respondents to 1967 SCOPE College Questionnaire. Eleven percent identified self as mixture of racial/ethnic groups or chose not to respond. Data adjusted by assigning ⅓ of this group to Negro, ⅓ to Caucasian, and ⅓ to "Other." Caucasian includes Mexican-American.

†SOURCE: Creager et al., 1968. Adjusted by rounding; adding ½ of "Other" to Negro because of black response to that term; and adding American Indian to "Other."

‡SOURCE: Cross, 1969. The 5 percent in the "Other" category has been added to Cross's reporting of these comparative Guidance and Placement Program data.

TABLE 15
Racial composition of enrollments in 11 large urban community colleges

State and college	Total enrollment	Percent		
		White	Negro	Other
California				
City College of San Francisco	12,438	71.1	10.8	18.1
Compton College	5,233	47.3	48.9	3.8
Contra Costa College (Richmond)	5,351	64.9	26.2	8.9
East Los Angeles College	13,136	54.6	5.3	40.1
Los Angeles City College	10,476	51.0	26.6	22.4
Merritt College (Oakland)	8,622	63.6	29.7	6.7
Ilinois				
Chicago City College	13,115	69.9	27.8	2.3
Michigan				
Flint Community College	6,558	86.6	15.0	0.4
Highland Park College	3,781	53.7	45.7	0.6
Missouri				
Junior College District of St. Louis	10,121	85.6	14.0	0.4
Texas				
El Centro (Dallas)	6,053	81.8	14.0	4.2
San Antonio College	12,717	46.5	11.1	42.4

SOURCE: *The Chronicle of Higher Education,* April 22, 1968 (based on data reported to the U.S. Office of Civil Rights by most colleges and universities).

data on the distribution and differentiation of the SCOPE seniors of 1966 after leaving high school. He offers the data presented in Table 14 on the racial make-up of the junior college population (Tillery, 1970).

Cross reports that across the nation, public community colleges enrolled a slightly lower proportion of Caucasians than did other types of institutions. SCOPE findings show that along with the non-Catholic church-related colleges of the South, the junior colleges were the least restrictive in reference to minority enrollments. In contrast, the independent universities and Catholic institutions were most restrictive, with the public universities somewhere in between the extremes.

Some urban community colleges nearly replicate the racial mix of their communities and enroll much higher ratios of minority students than indicated by national averages. Table 15 shows the enrollments and racial composition of several large community colleges in six states.

It is important to note that there are enormous regional differences in the way types of institutions serve nonwhite students. K. P. Cross, in her review (1969, pp. 20, 21) of relevant research, draws the following conclusions:

The South, for example, has far and away the largest number of Negro students in college, but only 6% are enrolled in public community colleges; 55% are enrolled in public 4-year colleges. Although the far western states have only about one-tenth as many Negro college students as the South, 70% of these are enrolled in public community colleges—probably in the extensive community college system of California.

There is widespread agreement that if minority youth are to have equal educational opportunities, the public community colleges must serve as bridges between high school and career employment for some and between high school and advanced higher education for others.

Noting that almost half of the 260,000 black students now in college are enrolled in predominantly Negro colleges, Bowles and DeCosta (1971) conclude that in the near future these institutions will enroll a minority of black students in higher education. In doing so, they see the public community colleges—which already enroll more black students than any other type of institution—as the primary source for equal opportunity in higher education:

. . . It is worth noting that the greatest attraction of this institution (community colleges) appears to be that they are urban, and usually have close ties with nearby, urban-oriented regional colleges to which their graduates transfer.

This interpretation of the pull of community colleges is congruent with current studies which document the rising educational aspirations not only of black students but of other ethnic groups—particularly those with Spanish-speaking backgrounds. All of these groups see the community college as a stepping-stone to even *higher* education. These rising aspirations of youth from ethnic groups are ill served by the schism between academic and occupational education in American education. The rejection of traditional vocational education by students of modest or impaired educational backgrounds disturbs many educators. For others it is a challenge to tear down the walls which divide education. This call for change is well stated in a recent working paper for the then United States Commissioner of Education (Feldman, 1969, p. 13):

If we are to meet our educational responsibilities to space-age youth, we can no longer tolerate an educational system that in large part ignores the concept of career education. A necessary first step is to redefine vocational education, at least in part, as that aspect of an educational experience which helps a person to discover, define, and refine his talents, and to use them in working toward a career. This definition sees vocational education embracing, but not confined to, development of manual skills; it sees such skills used not merely to prepare for tasks, but as alternatives or supplements to verbal skills in the entire learning process.

This point of view echoes the calls to make the community college a bridge between school and expanding opportunities. But it adds a note which is often neglected: "The essence of our new system is that at no point in time is any career choice or future foreclosed to any student by the school" (*ibid.,* p. 16). This has long been the philosophy of the community colleges, if not always their practice.

The high educational aspirations of minority students, of low as well as of high verbal ability, suggest the challenges ahead for all higher education, but especially for the two-year colleges (Froomkin, 1969). This is not only because of the *number* of "new students to higher education" who will be channeled there, but because of conflicts which will surely result from apparent incongruence between student aspiration and achievement.

There is already some unrest among minorities because of state plans which channel them into two-year institutions. Some of them do not see the local community college as a bridge to higher aspirations; nor do they see these colleges manned by teachers better prepared than most in higher education to help repair serious deficiencies in earlier education. Instead, they interpret state systems of coordinated institutions which send high-achieving students to senior colleges and the rest to junior colleges as racist in effect, if not in intent. This point of view does not appear to be widespread, however, and certainly is not reflected in findings that twice as many nonwhite students as white students plan to enter a two-year college as the first step in attaining a four-year degree (Froomkin, 1969).

The authors, on the basis of extensive associations with community college administrators and faculty leaders across the country, believe that these institutions will accept the challenge of serving the new students to higher education. The cry is now: "Help us find new ways to educate the undereducated and to be relevant to our students whose interests and backgrounds are unlike those of traditional college students. Above all, we need the resources in talent and money to do the job." Although the community colleges are serving more minority students than other public colleges and universities, equal opportunity in the "people's college" is only a partially fulfilled promise.

COMMUNITY OUTREACH The practice of outreach is not new to the junior colleges, nor was it to the land-grant colleges before them. The question is, who reaches out to whom? The most notable efforts in 1969 sought to reach alienated individuals, groups, and neighborhoods through programs conceived and carried out by persons who had shared in the experiences which alienate large segments of our cities from the main thrust of American society. The language, the look, and even the stated goals of these programs are new to higher education. Nevertheless, they clearly represent efforts to produce on the claims community colleges make about responding to the special needs of the communities which support them. The deficit in providing equal opportunities for *all* has been more a matter of priorities — and myopia — than of institutional philosophy. It is not surprising that many administrators and teachers would expect the ghetto to come to them at the very time that they reach out to serve the business and industrial segments of their communities. To be sure, traditional community service programs are helpful for those who seek occupational and personal renewal. But the preparation of the educationally neglected for the mainstream of community life has yet to become a major achievement of community colleges.

The new outreach tries to touch and motivate the alienated in unconventional ways and settings. A series of thumbnail sketches will convey the variety and potential of these programs.

Cleveland. Before the first permanent building was constructed, Cuyahoga College had "storefront" guidance centers in the black communities of the central city.

San Mateo. A largely white college went out to seek minority students and paid them to learn. Although the community college had difficulties living up to its promises, it recruited a talented and unconventional staff which "turned on" many ghetto students. This college was appraised as having the most effective of all California junior college programs for the undereducated (Berg and Axtell, 1968).

New York City. With support from the Office of Economic Opportunity and supervision from the American Association of

Junior Colleges, the Brooklyn Urban Center of CCNY is reaching out to serve the parents of Head Start children—to help them become involved in the education of their own children and to explore new careers for themselves.

Chicago. What is now Malcolm X College is taking English as a second language into the homes of black citizens and Spanish-speaking immigrants. In doing so, it is developing tutors and teachers from the minority communities served by the program.

Tucson. Under special grants from the United States Office of Education, the newly formed Pima Community College in Tucson assembled a core staff of administrators, faculty, and consultants in a year-long institute to develop an educational program and governance structure that would ensure relevant educational opportunities for the diverse youth and adults of the Tucson area. Particular attention is being given (1) to the employment of ethnic faculty and administrators in porportion to the ethnic characteristics of the community; and (2) to interdisciplinary programs which focus on the career and personal development of Pima students. Broad staff and community commitment to these goals has been furthered through the use of a panel of outside consultants.

Oakland. Perhaps the most complex and ambitious of the federally funded outreach programs is being conducted by the Peralta Junior College District by means of four centers in the surrounding poor communities. From its two urban campuses, corps of student workers and professional staffs at the centers seek to help blacks, Chicanos, and members of other ethnic groups in unconventional ways—short-term courses in legal rights, household management, English, child care, and an array of career and academic courses. Some of these activities take place in neighborhood agencies and churches, others at the centers, and, increasingly, on the parent campuses.

Recently, a multiracial team made a statement about outreach in the community colleges (Tillery et al., 1969, p. 7), which is a fitting summary of this section:

During the last decade or so, while junior colleges were being redefined as community colleges, there has been a din of brave words attesting to how these colleges would serve the communities' needs; would not only open their doors but would reach out to those most in need of education, in need of cultural identity, and in need of opportunity. The uncomfortable fact is that much of the rhetoric has been largely hollow. To be sure, the middle-class majority groups have been rather broadly served and there are community colleges with heavy enrollments from disadvantaged ethnic groups. Some have, in response to ethnic and political threats, modified traditional programs to meet unique needs. Not many, if any, have embarked on such a potentially ambitious outreach program as the Inner City Project of the Peralta Junior Colleges. . . . This tripartite experiment of the OEO, American Association of Junior Colleges, and Peralta Colleges has a good chance of evolving a viable model by which urban colleges can really serve the diverse communities within the metropolis.

EDUCATION OF THE UNDER-EDUCATED No other segment of American higher education has given anything like the attention and resources the public junior colleges have devoted to the task of healing the wounds caused by deficient and bad education. It has taken courage for these colleges to define their quality by what they can do for students who need help, rather than by what students can bring to them from the competitive market of high achievers.

"Remedial" education has generally been less successful, according to Berg (1965), and is now a nasty word among many educators as well as minority students. Even though the labels are being changed (basic?—tutorial?—readiness?), the problems remain. The poor reader cannot realize his aspiration to be a lawyer until he learns to read. The girl who fears mathematics cannot enter a nursing major until she has learned basic arithmetic. Her girlfriend is just as seriously handicapped in becoming a secretary because her spelling is at the grade school level. And finally, the black youth who is concerned about his identity doesn't see the point to endless drills in the remedial three R's. He stops trying, and fails to complete his first semester. Because large numbers of junior college students lack specific skills necessary for acceptable achievement in college-level courses, great numbers of remedial sections are offered each semester in writing, arithmetic, reading, and study habits.

The less-than-college-level courses have proved onerous to students and teachers alike. Furthermore, many remedial programs have failed to take into consideration the underlying problems of motivation. For example, it has been common practice to grade students in remedial classes not on individual progress but, instead, against the standards of college-level courses. This can scarcely be defended even if large numbers of these students should move on, for example, into the traditional English and mathematics courses, which they do not. This problem is clearly reflected in the data on anachronistic grading presented by DeHart (1964).

This president's concern was not only for the negative motivation resulting from grading practices in the remedial English sections, but for the inconsistency of grading standards. With some coolness he observed that ". . . English 200 . . . was taught in 12 sections; one section had a low success index (C grade or above) of 9%, while . . . one section had a 54% success index, and the median for the 12 sections was 34%." Along with other examples, he concludes that such grading practices are "not easy to explain in rational terms" (*ibid.,* pp. 51–53).

Self-identity, motivation, and idiosyncratic barriers to learning come closer to the real problems of the undereducated than the need for remedial work. It is likely that the compelling demands of ethnic minority groups for "relevant" education have shattered the molds of traditional remedial programs. Such a hypothesis is to be intensively studied at the Center for Research and Development in Higher Education at the University of California, Berkeley, to shed light on the impact of ethnic programs on institutional structures—curriculum, governance, and student services. Although still competing for resources and faculty support, the *new* efforts at remediation stress individual tutoring, ethnic studies, and supportive workshops for students experiencing difficulties in regular courses. Such changes seem to be motivating teachers, as well as students, to learn.

SCOPE findings, to date, suggest that many junior college youths are marginal students, not only because of economic pressures and lack of incentives at home, but because they themselves are not sure they can make it. Compared to their peers in senior colleges, they have had only modest success in high school, less than satisfying guidance experiences, and continuing doubts about their ability to do college work. From Chart 11 it is clear that whereas 71 percent of the 1966 SCOPE seniors who went to independent universities *definitely* believed they could do college work, 71 percent of the public junior college students had doubts about their capabilities. It is likely that many of the junior college group who said they "probably had the ability" were expressing overconfidence (Tillery, 1970–71).

The self-doubts, the reluctance to try, the all-too-ready admission

CHART 11 *Distribution of student's self-estimation of ability to do college work for groups who went to three types of institutions. Four states.*

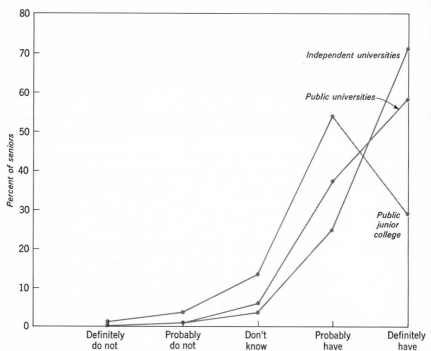

SOURCE: Tillery, 1970–71, SCOPE Project, Center for Research and Development in Higher Education, University of California, Berkeley.

of failure—all these manifestations of student vulnerability have been exacerbated by the red-pencil syndrome of remedial courses. The new look in developmental education is long overdue, but the early appraisals of innovative approaches to educating the under-educated is promising (Berg and Axtell, 1968; Johnson, 1969). In reporting "success for marginal students" the faculty team at Macomb County Community College concluded that their "first three years of operation have led the program into the area of student self-concept and self-fulfilling prophecy; this is becoming the new direction of the program. . . . [The program] is geared to help students believe they really can make it in college; therefore, vocational redirection is no longer a program goal" (Chalghian, 1969, p. 30).

THE URBAN COMMUNITY COLLEGE OF THE 70s Among the public community colleges which are being established weekly across the nation are some which seek to offer new relevance in serving the inner city, with its seething pressures from poorly educated migrants of various ethnic groups from rural America who are not prepared for either economic or cultural survival in the cities (Hauser, 1966). These campuses are in the inner city.

One such college is to be in the heart of downtown Miami. Under a president who is willing to experiment and a young director willing to risk his career, the new institution seeks to become something new and distinctive—it may have the community college look of the future.

The concept for this new community college resulted from days of work by teachers, students, architects, administrators, neighborhood activists, and city officials—of all ages and colors.

The Downtown Campus in Miami seeks to become (Fryer, 1969, pp. 2-4)

. . . a campus totally committed to serving the needs of *individuals* and collectivities in its community. . . . [I]t must find ways to adapt itself to the uniqueness of each of its students, rather than making itself . . . an impersonal obstacle course through which students must compete . . . against each other. . . . [T]he new campus must screen people in, not out. . . . [T]he new campus must be intent upon the human condition . . . choosing to respond to the validity of each person's need *as* it exists, *where* it exists.

. . . a campus which takes pains to communicate to all people. . . . [I]t is for them. . . . [S]tructures must invite the city and its people to come in . . . rather than walling them out.

. . . a campus which in many ways is indistinguishable from the [central] city it serves . . . but an identifiable home base and a source of support for those who need it.

. . . The new campus should set out to intervene in the processes of urban deterioration [and contribute to] the city's efforts at self-renewal . . . a center of educational, intellectual, and cultural enrichment. . . .

. . . an experimental campus . . . a laboratory using research evidence, introspection, and response from its community . . . in a constant process of change and self-renewal.

. . . The campus model of governance must be democratic, based on participation in decision-making by all those affected by the outcomes of decisions.

. . . a campus which attempts to recruit and retain sensitive faculty and staff who are concerned people of high energy, commitment, and learning. . . . [It will need] its staff as *ends* as well as means.

. . . a public agency . . . which seeks efficient and effective ways of investing funds so that the public receives maximum return . . . careful coordination within the college . . . and with relevant community organizations and agencies.

The goals of the junior college have always been idealistic and an influence for the democratization of higher education. The new urban community colleges grow from this tradition, but they seek to respond to the desperate needs of urban man. In coordination with other institutions of education, community groups, and government, these changing colleges offer hope for the nation's cities.

6. A Staff for the Task

The junior college has long prided itself on good student-faculty-administrative relationships, concern for the individual student, close articulation with secondary schools, and excellent teaching. The performance of its transfer students and the favorable testimony of its former students, as reflected in innumerable studies of alumni, lead to the conclusion that it has an enviable record. However, the characteristics, preparation, working conditions, and compensation of personnel have been cause for concern.

Staffing the burgeoning junior colleges has become big business. Of the total gross staff of approximately 96,000 for both public and private junior colleges reported in the 1969 *Directory* of the American Association of Junior Colleges (AAJC) for the academic year 1967–68, more than 84,000 were faculty, and more than 11,000 were administrators. The total faculty that year represented more than a 375 percent increase over what it was in 1957–58. Obviously, the growth has only begun, and, as discussed later in this chapter, the crucial problems now have to do with the recruitment, preparation, and appropriate utilization of staff for the coming decade.

FACULTY CHARACTERISTICS Who are the junior college teachers, and what are their backgrounds? Some of the answers come from a study of a stratified sample of 57 community colleges throughout the country. In one phase of the study, information was collected on more than 4,000 staff members. The findings from that study are supplemented by data from other sources. From the various studies it is possible to make the following generalizations:

The community college staff is composed primarily of those in the 31- to 50-year-old age bracket. Fewer than 18 percent in the study were under 30, and only 23 percent were over 50.

The master's degree is the highest one held by most members of the staff. Of those in the national sample, 77.7 percent held an M.A. or M.S. degree. Only 8.6 percent held a doctorate. Slightly more than 10 percent had earned only a bachelor's, and only 3.5 percent were working on less than a bachelor's. These data correspond closely with what Beazley reported about the highest degree held by the 1966 estimated full-time teaching and research staff in public two-year colleges in the United States: doctor's, 5.9 percent; master's, 74.9 percent; bachelor's or lower, 18.4 percent; and first professional, 1 percent (Beazley, 1966).

Data reported in Table 16 for the state of Illinois differentiate between the degree status of faculty in baccalaureate-oriented, occupational, and adult education curricula (Anderson & Thornblod, 1969).

The Illinois data are for all full-time and part-time staff, hence they are not exactly comparable to the two national samples. However, the information about Illinois faculty members is helpful in two respects. In the first place, the distinction between faculty degree preparation in the two types of curricula is important. The relatively large number of faculty recruited to teach in the vocational-technical field who possess only a bachelor's degree or less is understandable in view of the emphasis in such fields on work experience (in comparison with academic preparation). But even when that distinction is made, the high proportion of faculty members holding an M.A. degree characterizes the educational attainment of the group as a whole. The other significant feature of the Illinois data is the separate "Master's plus 30" category, which characterizes community college faculty who have pursued graduate work well beyond the M.A. yet have not earned a doctorate. It has been estimated that as much as one-fourth of all faculty

TABLE 16 Highest degree attained by teaching faculty, Illinois public junior colleges (by percent)	Doctorate	Master's plus 30	Master's	Bachelor's	Less than bachelor's
In baccalaureate programs	6	26	63	4	1
In occupational and adult education curricula	2	13	45	26	14
All teaching staff	4	21	56	13	6

SOURCE: Board for Higher Education, State of Illinois.

in public two-year colleges are in this category. The willingness of junior college staff members to pursue further study to this extent reinforces the current proposals for creating a nonresearch doctorate for teachers.

Community college faculty are recruited from a wide variety of sources. In the study of the 57 institutions, staff members were asked to indicate their principal occupation immediately before their current college position. By far the largest number—almost one-third of the total—came from the public school system, usually as teachers, counselors, or administrators from high schools. The next largest group, approximately 22 percent, were directly from graduate school. Next in line was the group, accounting for 11 percent of the total, who were recruited from four-year institutions. Approximately 10 percent came from business or industry and the remainder from a variety of other sources. In a study of the backgrounds of over 1,300 new full-time faculty members employed in the California community colleges in September, 1967, Phair (1968–1969) found that 36 percent were experienced secondary school teachers. The next largest group, amounting to 19 percent of the total, was composed of individuals who transferred from one junior college to another. Fifteen percent came directly from teaching positions in four-year colleges or universities. Approximately 11 percent were recruited from industry, and another 9 percent, many of them from graduate school, came with no teaching experience.

A high proportion of community college faculty members are new to their institutions. In the national study conducted by the Center, over 46 percent of the staff members of the 57 established institutions had been employed by their college for a period ranging between one and three years. Nineteen percent fell within the range of four to six years.

Only a minority of community college staff members were oriented to the institution by reason of having once been students in such institutions or by having completed a course or courses dealing specifically with community colleges. In the national study approximately 8 percent had once been students in the community college for one year or less, and another 20 percent had been students for more than one year. When asked whether they had completed a course or courses on the community college, only one-third responded affirmatively.

No specific data are readily available, but a general impression exists that relatively few junior college faculty members are from minority ethnic groups and that the social class background of many white staff members makes it difficult for them to relate to students from various ethnic groups. This situation is also found in most other schools and colleges, but it is particularly critical in the case of the junior college, in which so many minority group students enroll. Naturally the problem has many implications for the recruiting and training of faculty members and administrators from other than middle-class backgrounds.

Although no attempt is made here to compare faculty in two- and four-year colleges, certain differences, especially those with respect to previous experience and educational attainment, are readily apparent. This does not, however, give cause for concern, because the nature and function of the two-year institutions are in many ways different from those of four-year colleges and universities. While the latter are obviously concerned about good under-graduate teaching—perhaps more so now than ever before—most of them are also involved with research and graduate education, and thus their faculty requirements are different. Moreover, the community college's involvement in vocational education, as indicated above, means that it must recruit certain faculty members with skills and backgrounds peculiar to teaching in that area.

ISSUES AND PROBLEMS   Several issues and problems with respect to staff are emphasized here because of their particular significance for the future of the public community college.

Attitudes of Faculty toward the Institution   Over the years a great deal of concern has been expressed about whether junior college teachers are really in harmony with the avowed purposes of their institutions. Medsker (1960) called attention to the fact that faculty members, in line with the theory of "reference groups," may consider themselves more closely related to a group to which they aspire to belong rather than to the junior college family of which they are actually members. In the recent national study of the 57 community colleges, referred to previously, faculty members were asked several questions about teaching in the community college and about the proper functions of such an institution.

While 53.8 percent of respondents indicated that they preferred to be employed in a community college, 26.7 percent said they would prefer to be employed at a four-year college, and 17.7 percent specified that they would prefer to be employed in a university. While the pecking order of prestige among institutions might be expected to lead to such a distribution of responses, the fact that so many staff members would really prefer to be elsewhere at least raises a question as to the institutional commitment found in the community college.

The staff members were also asked to indicate whether they believed that certain types of educational programs were "essential," "optional," or "inappropriate" for the community college. The responses revealed a tendency to favor the more traditional aspects of college and to question many of the special services which the community colleges are presumed to render. As revealed in Table 13 (Chapter 4), most of the staff said it was essential for the college to offer both a transfer program and standard two-year technical curricula, but when less conventional programs were considered, the responses were not nearly so universal. Only 50 percent felt that occupational curricula for skilled and semi-skilled trades were essential, and only about a fifth of the group thought the college should be concerned with occupational programs of less than two years' duration. Only about one-half of the respondents thought that remedial courses were essential. About one-third thought such courses should be optional, and almost 16 percent said they were inappropriate. Questions about other unique community college offerings and services revealed the same tendency. Almost one-half of the respondents thought that too much stress is placed on the *quantity* of students and not enough on *quality*. As might be expected, the nature of responses varied among staff members with different responsibilities and backgrounds. Counselors and administrators were generally more flexible in their attitudes concerning the program than were teachers. Teachers of academic subjects were more traditional in their points of view than were those who taught in applied fields. And those who said that they would prefer to teach in a four-year college or university were more likely to oppose occupational and remedial programs.

The problem reflected by staff attitudes is serious because if the staff is not in harmony with the expectations held for the community college, those expectations may not be realized. A study of attitudes in any type of educational institution might reveal no greater degree of harmony than was indicated by the study of community colleges, but since the functions, program, and services of the community college are so diverse, it is particularly essential that those who work in it not be rejecting of the goals of the institution. Obviously, the situation has implications for the recruitment, preparation, and in-service training of staff.

Determining an Optimum Work Load
A growing problem in the expanding community colleges has been the unavoidable proliferation of faculty responsibilities. Many faculty members indicate that there is inadequate time available to perform properly the academic duties for which they are responsible. Teachers in junior colleges carry heavier class loads than do those in four-year institutions and thus are subject to a comparatively unfavorable faculty-student ratio. This has generally been rationalized on the basis that faculty in the junior college are not expected to engage in research, nor do they deal with upper-division and graduate students whose needs are presumed to be more exacting than those of lower-division students. Perhaps, too, the historical affiliation of the community college with the secondary school led to teaching loads roughly commensurate with those in high school. One rough measure of teaching loads is the number of teaching hours per week, which until recently tended to be in the 15–18 hour range—with some allowance on the lower side for "lecture" courses and a slightly higher load when much of the work was in a laboratory situation. Gradually the loads were examined, and adjustments were made for teachers in fields such as English, where heavy writing assignments required more than ordinary time for evaluation.

A more realistic measure is the figure for weekly student contact hours per full-time faculty member, which takes into consideration the number of students under a teacher's jurisdiction. In a study of faculty load conducted in 1968 for the San Jose (California) City College by the Field Service Center at the University of California at Berkeley, data on this measure were gathered from several California community colleges. The study staff recommended that the college should work toward a 500 weekly student contact hour load per FTE (full-time-equivalent) faculty, but that there should be legitimate variations among programs and faculty.

Today, demands from teacher organizations, particularly union groups, are resulting in negotiation on faculty load as well as on other working conditions. One of the most drastic teaching-load revisions effected was at Chicago City College in early 1969. There, under severe pressure from the Teachers' Union, the college agreed to reduce both the class-hour load and class size. The load established for all teachers was 12 contact hours per week. This, together with a sizable reduction in class size, brought the average teacher-student ratio for all campuses to a low of 1 to 19.08. Previously, the ratio had ranged from 1 to 22 to 1 to 23.

The American Association of Junior Colleges has made the following rough estimates of the trend in *faculty-student ratio* from data on enrollments and faculty reported in its *Directory:* 1965 — 1 to 26.6; 1966 — 1 to 24.2; 1967 — 1 to 22.8; 1968 — 1 to 22.0; 1969 — 1 to 23.0. No explanation is given for the increase estimated for 1969, although the use of gross data in making rough calculations could easily lead to variation. Nonetheless, the general downward trend is apparent.

Obviously, such a trend has widespread implications for institutional costs and also constitutes a variable to be reckoned with in projecting future faculty needs. While the Chicago situation is not representative of the teaching load throughout the country, it may point to fewer classes and clock hours of teaching time per week. On the other hand, there seems little likelihood that such loads will soon resemble those found in most four-year institutions.

The community college faculty member, unlike his four-year college and university counterpart, must work with larger numbers of heterogeneous students and must consequently be prepared to offer diversified programs of instruction including beginning, advanced, general, transfer, remedial, and terminal courses. To accommodate the many and varied students enrolled in the two-year institution, the faculty member must continually review relevant literature and materials in order to update and prepare course materials and teaching aids relevant to his students' needs.

Class loads and class size directly influence the type of educational opportunities faculty members afford students and relate to the extent of learning taking place in the classroom. This point of view is well documented in Garrison's study of junior college teachers and their problems (Garrison, 1967). He said teachers contended that their problems included inadequate time to do their jobs, a need for professional refreshment and affiliation, a role in college government, and a need to be less isolated from one another as groups and as individuals within separate disciplines. He further wrote:

There is not enough time, the teachers said, to keep up in my own field; to develop innovations or new methods in my own teaching; to do a proper job with individual students; to investigate what other junior colleges are doing; to study for myself; to discuss educational matters with my fellow-teachers; even, more often than I like to think, to do a decent job of preparation for my classes; to refresh myself, even occasionally, by brief association with some of my colleagues in my own discipline, whether at conventions, special regional meetings, or whatever; to function effectively on faculty committees; to help in advising student organizations.

Traditionally, there have been no generally acceptable guidelines with which critics of faculty work loads can measure faculty productivity or justify reduced class loads to help teachers prepare to meet changing junior college student needs. Currently there is increasing concern by faculty and administrators to develop reasonable solutions to the problems of measuring junior college teaching loads. While there is no simple solution to the class load measurement problem, numerous attempts are being made by educators and others to equalize faculty assignments and responsibilities.

Compensation of Faculty While the salaries of faculty members in public two-year colleges have increased materially in the last few years, there is still a question of whether they are sufficiently high to attract the number of high-caliber teachers needed. A recent survey by the National Education Association (1968) revealed that the median annual salary in approximately 500 of these institutions for the academic year 1967–68 was $9,165. The faculties of about 5 percent of these institutions received $13,500 or more a year, 11.6 percent received $12,500 or above, and 4.7 percent received less than $6,500. As would be expected, there were differences among regions, with the colleges in the far West paying considerably more than those located in the southeastern part of the nation.

A comparison of salaries in public two-year colleges with those in nonpublic institutions reveals that the private colleges are severely disadvantaged. The NEA survey revealed that in 153 nonpublic institutions the median annual salary was $7,211— almost $2,000 less than in the public institutions. In the nonpublic colleges only 5.9 percent of the faculty received $10,000 or more, 25 percent received $8,242 or more, 25 percent received $6,447 or more, and 4.1 percent received less than $5,000.

It is difficult to compare salaries paid to faculty in two-year colleges with those in four-year institutions. One reason for this is that most of the four-year colleges and universities utilize the system of academic rank in the employment and promotion of faculty, whereas this system is not used in many of the two-year institutions. Salary data for the four-year colleges are reported by rank. The NEA survey reported that for 1967–68 median salaries by the various categories of rank in the four-year institutions were as follows:

Instructors and lecturers	$ 7,496
Assistant professors	9,472
Associate professors	11,393
Professors	14,713

The median salary of *all* full-time teaching personnel in four-year institutions was $10,235.

It is clear that teaching salaries in public two-year colleges tend to compare favorably with those in four-year institutions at the assistant professor level, but the two-year colleges severely lag behind in maximum rates for those with advanced rank.

Undoubtedly, part of the difference in salaries between the two types of institutions is accounted for by differences in qualification as measured by degrees held and also by differences in criteria for promotion. Only a relatively small percentage of junior college faculty hold doctoral degrees, but the reverse is true for faculty members in four-year institutions. The instructional staff in many of the public two-year colleges are appointed and promoted on the basis of degrees held, previous teaching experience, and length of tenure in the particular college. While the same factors are present in part in the four-year colleges, others, such as amount and quality of research efforts and publications, constitute additional important criteria, particularly for promotion, and thus affect salaries in ways not found in many junior colleges.

In recent years, faculty members in two-year institutions have accelerated their demand for fringe benefits and, to a large extent, have been successful in obtaining them. Thus in recent years junior colleges have increased retirement benefits, improved sabbatical leave privileges, and have initiated health and dental plans.

How far junior colleges can go in raising salaries and increasing fringe benefits is a question with many implications. To argue against higher compensation regardless of its form would seem to argue against quality teaching and adequate teacher supply. On the other hand, the willingness of the public to support public community colleges will be based in part on its interpretation of their reasonableness in overall costs. However, faculty positions in community colleges must be made increasingly attractive, and it seems unreasonable that the differential between salaries in public and private two-year colleges and in four-year institutions should be as great as it is.

Academic Rank Although it is difficult to ascertain the number of junior colleges using academic rank, increasing numbers of them are adopting such a system. Nevertheless, many educators believe that the two-year college should carefully consider its function and mission before moving toward a reward system so closely associated with the university model. A system of academic rank and the effect its adoption might have on the type and quality of instruction provided in the junior college is of particular concern. The issue boils down to the question of what real advantages or disadvantages faculty ranking provides. Historically, rank has been associated with academic merit, scholarly research, and publication. Advocates of academic ranking say that it adds prestige, facilitates recruitment and retention of faculty members, stimulates and rewards professional growth, increases psychological identification with the community of higher education, and increases faculty status and morale.

In an article entitled "Academic Rank—Promise or Peril," Tillery (1963) contends that professorial rank is identified with the traditions of scholarship and the advancement of the frontiers of knowledge, but that a junior college faculty structure should be based on very different but equally worthy goals. If junior college structure is to be nontraditional, a question arises as to whether a two-year college can best serve its purpose by adopting the traditional ranking system of the four-year college and university.

Hendrix (1963–1964, and 1965) investigated the ways in which faculty members in junior colleges without academic rank policies and procedures differ from those in junior colleges with such policies and procedures. He later wrote:

Academic rank policies and procedures are associated with some desirable characteristics, but are also uniquely related to sufficient undesirable characteristics to cast suspicion on the advisability of such policies for the public junior college. . . . The presence or absence of academic rank policies appears not only to differentiate faculty characteristics but also affects the environment (curricular and extracurricular) as it is perceived by students. It should be remembered that it is the environment of which the student is aware that largely determines the way in which he functions in a college.

If the community colleges are to meet the cultural, educational, social, and vocational needs of the community, the advantages and disadvantages of academic rank should be carefully reviewed before being accepted as a part of the community college image. This is particularly important today when this institution enrolls an increasing number of students who are unfamiliar with and unaccustomed to the rank and status of professorial titles traditionally associated with four-year institutions.

Preparation of Faculty
Faculty preparation for junior college teaching is extremely important. Good teaching is said to characterize these institutions, and an enormous number of faculty members must be recruited for the expanding numbers of public two-year colleges. The problem of faculty preparation may be divided into two parts: preservice and in-service.

Preservice

The fact that, historically, the public community college was considered an extension of the secondary school meant that initially, in most of the states, credential requirements imposed by state departments of education dictated a certain amount of professional preparation for junior college teaching. While the professional requirement was often supplemented by prescriptions as to minimum subject matter preparation, the requirements with regard to professional courses often dominated. The advent of the public two-year college as a system divorced from the public schools has almost eliminated the credential requirement or at least has placed increasing emphasis on subject-matter preparation.

This situation gives rise to concern as to whether those entering community college teaching are sufficiently oriented to the task of dealing with an exceedingly diverse student population. An understanding of the mission and scope of the community college and of how students with varying motivational, interest, and ability patterns learn is essential. This in no way detracts from the importance of competence in subject matter. How to achieve these multiple goals is a dilemma both for those who plan and administer community colleges, and for those in teacher training institutions who are concerned with the preparation of college faculty. It appears that in recent years the preparation of teachers for this level of education has been limited primarily to preparation in subject matter. Cooper (1964) indicated that the major obstacle to the development of programs for the training of community college teachers is that there has been no clear-cut allocation of responsibility for this task.

Despite this situation, however, many signs point to a revival of interest in the problem. In April, 1967, more than 200 colleges and universities indicated interest in preparing college teachers, and many intended to establish programs especially designed for junior college instructors. The American Association of Junior Colleges indicated later that during 1969, 75 to 100 graduate institutions offered an identifiable graduate program designed to include preparation of new, career-oriented, junior college faculty in one or more recognized disciplines. Several new programs of preparing junior college teachers are under way. The Southern Illinois University and the Junior College District of St. Louis are now cooperating on an internship program in the preparation of teachers in occupational programs. The University of Miami has initiated a degree known as the Diplomate in College Teaching which extends two years beyond the baccalaureate and one year beyond the master's. Miami State Junior College works closely with the local university in an advisory capacity and in providing teaching internships for the program. The University of California at Berkeley, under the jurisdiction of the Junior College Leadership Program, has a cooperative internship program with some 20 community colleges for the preparation of beginning teachers. A special feature of the program is an emphasis on the recruitment and preparation of individuals from minority groups. As a means of attracting the interest of junior college administrators and of disseminating information concerning the development of programs for preservice preparation and in-service training of junior college teachers, the American Association of Junior Colleges held a conference at Airlie House, Virginia in November, 1968. Those attending this symposium concluded that stereotyped ideas concerning junior college faculty preparation and in-service training "aren't good enough any more," and indicated a need for plurality in the types of teacher training and the types of institutions providing it. Accordingly, various models for instructor preparation and training were proposed or reviewed. These included various forms of a Doctor of Arts program leading to college teaching; a program in which junior colleges themselves establish and administer one or more institutions for the preparation of instructors; various forms of intrainstitutional cooperation; and a two-year post-baccalaureate specialist program. The Education Professions Development Act provides encouragement for such new approaches to the preparation of junior college teachers and counselors.

Quite aside from the structural aspects of the various current or proposed models is the question of which particular elements are necessary in the preparation of faculty. Among those that seem particularly relevant are the following: the history of the two-year college and its place in American higher education; modern learning theory, including the uses and limits of educational evaluation, testing, and measurements; the characteristics and values of the diverse student population at today's junior colleges; an opportunity for supervised teaching or internship at a two-year college; a knowledge of modern media and new techniques of instruction.

Whether two-year colleges will or should employ an increasing number of teachers holding doctorates is a moot question at this time. The growing number of individuals with such a degree who appear to have difficulty in obtaining employment could lead many of them to seek and obtain positions in junior colleges. However, persuasive arguments can be advanced for specifically designed programs to prepare junior college teachers. There are new demands for such programs growing out of an increasing awareness of the dangers inherent in a system which recruits faculty who are neither familiar with, nor concerned about, the role of the community college, who have no concept concerning the nature of its student body, and who are unaware of learning theories and means of evaluation.

In-service training
Even if the majority of future junior college teachers were to be recruited from well-conceived special training programs, their need

for professional growth after employment would continue. Faculty will be recruited from many additional sources, and those long on the job will have the usual problems with respect to keeping up with their subject fields. Thus, the need for well-conceived in-service programs grows greater each year. Although many administrators admit to this need and annually resolve to do something about it, the pressure of time and other problems seems to reduce the incidence of such programs to a minimum. It may be that the teacher training institutions themselves will have to assume a major responsibility for devising cooperative projects with community college districts for in-service training programs.

Whether formally planned or not, the potential for cooperation between local districts and nearby four-year colleges and universities appears to be both necessary and real. The costs of such ventures must, of course, be borne by someone, and they may indeed be a responsibility of the districts themselves. One way of assuring developments along this line would be for the state agencies responsible for community colleges to assume leadership in statewide plans that would facilitate cooperative arrangements between districts and teacher training institutions.

Projection of Staff Needs A number of uncontrolled variables enter into any projection of the future need for faculty members and administrators. The base, which itself is an estimate, obviously is the number of students to be accommodated. Beyond that, there are trends in the expected faculty-student ratio, the teacher class or clock hour load, and the nature of the educational program.

Based upon full-time-equivalent enrollment, projection C (Chapter 2), made by the Carnegie Commission, rough estimates have been made of faculty needs in public community colleges for the next decade. As reported earlier, projected FTE enrollment in junior colleges by 1975 is approximately 2.1 million students, and by 1980 it is predicted to be over 2.6 million. Two different assumptions were made about faculty-student ratio. One was that present trends toward a lower ratio would continue and would stabilize at 1 to 20. The other was that, due to the further development and utilization of teaching technologies, tutorials, and independent study, the ratio might eventually increase to a high of 1 to 25.

Several aspects of faculty needs during the 1970s are projected in Table 17. Estimates are made for total FTE as well as for the

		Estimated FTE faculty†			
		1975 faculty-student ratio		1980 faculty-student ratio	
Major field	FTE faculty,* 1966	1 : 20	1 : 25	1 : 20	1 : 25
Biological sciences	2,000	5,501	4,370	6,580	5,295
Business and commerce	4,000	11,002	8,741	13,162	10,591
English and journalism	5,300	14,579	11,581	17,440	14,034
Fine and applied arts	3,100	8,527	6,774	10,200	8,208
Foreign languages and literature	1,500	4,126	3,278	4,936	3,972
Health professions	1,200	3,301	2,622	3,949	3,177
Mathematics	2,600	7,152	5,681	8,555	6,885
Physical and health education	2,200	6,052	4,807	7,240	5,826
Physical sciences	2,500	6,877	5,463	8,227	6,620
Social sciences	4,000	11,002	8,740	13,162	10,591
Trade and industrial	4,100	11,278	8,959	13,491	10,856
All other fields	6,400	17,603	13,984	21,058	16,945
Total full-time-equivalent faculty	38,900	107,000	85,000	128,000	103,000

TABLE 17 Estimated full-time-equivalent faculty needs by major fields—1975 and 1980, based on a variable faculty-student ratio in public community colleges

*From estimates made by the Carnegie Commission on Higher Education.
†See Table 18 for estimated faculty needs from 1970 to 1975 and to 1980.

total number of faculty members needed by 1975 and 1980. Thus, by 1980 a total of 128,000 individuals may be needed if the ratio stabilizes at 1 to 20, whereas 103,000 would be required at the higher ratio of 1 to 25. Based on the requirements for 1970, this would mean an increase by 1980 in new faculty of either 59,000 or 47,000, depending on the faculty-student ratio. It is necessary, however, to allow also for replacements due to separations, retirements, and deaths, and when this is considered, an additional 30,000 or 24,000 will need to be recruited, thus making the total additional faculty either 89,000 or 71,000 by 1980.

Another assumption was that the present distribution of faculty members (on an FTE basis) by *major field* would remain reasonably constant. While such an assumption may not be entirely correct due to the need for the community college to become increasingly flexible, and also due to shifts in the total occupational patterns in the United States which have obvious implications for the com-

	1975 faculty-student ratio		1980 faculty-student ratio	
	1 : 20	1 : 25	1 : 20	1 : 25
Total full-time-equivalent faculty	107,000	85,000	128,000	103,000
Estimated total faculty†	118,000	94,000	140,000	113,000
New FTE faculty	32,000	26,000	54,000	43,000
Total new faculty	35,000	29,000	59,000	47,000
Replacement faculty‡	15,000	12,000	30,000	24,000
Total additional faculty needed	50,000	41,000	89,000	71,000

*These estimations are based on projection C of equivalent full-time enrollments shown in Table 7.

†Since FTE faculty do account for most faculty needed for part-time programs, only 10 percent of FTE faculty of 1970 has been added and rounded to thousands.

‡An average teacher longevity of 25 years is assumed in estimating replacements.

SOURCE: Compiled by authors from data supplied by the Carnegie Commission on Higher Education.

munity college curriculum, it at least leads to a rough approximation of faculty needs by fields.

Table 18 reports the projections by fields for 1975 and 1980 based on the foregoing assumptions. Baseline data on FTE faculty by fields for 1966 were obtained from unpublished information in the United States Office of Education and are regarded as conservative. It is, of course, entirely possible that certain of the fields will require numbers in excess of those projected. A case in point is that of the health professions, since many prognosticators predict a nationwide emphasis on the preparation of additional workers in the allied health fields at all levels.

It goes without saying that the most difficult problem with respect to future faculty needs lies with the necessity to find men and women—many of them from ethnic minority groups—who can relate to the "new" student bodies in community colleges and to the institutions' exciting missions. It may prove to be relatively easy to find enough individuals to fill the slots but increasingly difficult to recruit the *right* people so that the community college can deliver on its commitments.

New Administrators   Estimating the number of community college *administrators* needed for the future is quite another matter, although here, too, the variables do not remain constant. In 1965, Schultz predicted that the average number of new administrators of junior colleges (public and private) per year would be as follows:

	Chief administrators	Chief administrative deans	Chief student personnel administrators	Chief business officers
1965–70	82.2	86.8	54.8	61.4
1970–75	95.2	101.6	65.0	70.2
1975–80	103.2	113.0	71.4	76.6

In 1968, Schultz reported that in 1966 and 1967 the actual numbers of new chief administrators were 161 and 165 and respectively—nearly double his earlier estimate by year during this period. He attributed the excess to the far greater number of new institutions that opened in those years (56 in 1966 and 72 in 1967) than he originally estimated. Naturally, the number of new administrators needed annually is tied closely to the number of new institutions, although as Schultz documented in his studies, the need is augmented substantially by replacements.

In the light of new projections for the community college during the 1970s it appears that Schultz's projections are still too conservative. Assuming that 280 new institutions will be established during the decade, a like number of new chief administrators will obviously be needed. In addition, based on a possible longevity period of 15 years, at least an additional 600 administrators would be required for replacements, thus bringing the possible total to nearly 900.

It is probable that even larger numbers of additional chief administrators to serve in instruction and student personnel will be needed. As present institutions increase in size, additional administrative officers to carry the load of work brought about by such growth will add to the total required for new institutions and for replacements. Fortunately, with funds made available by the W. K. Kellogg Foundation, a number of universities have, over the last decade, established centers for the preparation of administrators for the community colleges. These centers have added substantially to the supply and quality of community college administrators at all levels and in addition have aided the individual colleges in many ways.

IN SUMMARY The staffing problem is complex and continuing, and no single solution should be anticipated. Optimum utilization of faculty must be the joint concern of local and state level governing boards, administrators, and faculty. Problems of recruitment and preparation necessitate increasing attention on the part of the profession, state level agencies, the federal government, and the teacher preparation institutions.

7. Control and Support of Community Colleges

The community colleges are organized and supported in more varied and complex ways than are any other institutions of public postsecondary education. No single national pattern characterizes their governance. Their very title implies a local orientation and that they have had a legal affiliation with some type of local tax district. At their beginnings and for a good many years thereafter, they were an integral part of local public school systems. Legislation in 1917 made it possible in California for separate districts to be organized solely for the purpose of maintaining community colleges. While this form of organization became increasingly popular in other states, it did not become the dominant local structure until recent years. Meanwhile, many authorities continued to look with favor on the community college as an integral part of a local secondary school system, arguing that this would lead to a high degree of integration between high school and college. In fact, at one time a structure known as the 6-4-4 plan seemed to take hold. Under this plan an entire public school system was organized so that it included a six-year elementary school, a four-year intermediate unit through grade 10, and a top four-year unit consisting of the upper two years of high school and the first two of college.

In the process of evolution still another form emerged, namely, regional two-year institutions fully controlled and maintained by the state. This plan was adopted in some states as a means of ensuring the existence of two-year colleges which had not been, or presumably would not be, established when left to local initiative.

Because each state has responsibility for its own educational system, it is not surprising that a variety of forms for the provision of such a new and rapidly developing institution as the community college should emerge. Today two basic state patterns prevail: (1) situations in which the responsibility for the community colleges is shared between local and state government, and (2) those in which this responsibility rests primarily with the state. There are, however, a few states within which some of the community colleges are maintained under one plan and others under another. A variation is found in several states, where there are two-year branches maintained by major universities which are classified as community colleges. In some instances these exist alongside regular community colleges.

More confusing still is the variety of state-level agencies which are responsible for community colleges. To the extent that community colleges have been maintained by some type of local district, like all local schools they have been subjected to varying degrees of control and coordination by some state agency, historically a state board of education or a state department of public instruction.

Organizational diversity is apparent in Table 19, which shows the various states using the two basic plans, as well as those using the university control plan, and which also indicates the type of state board which has jurisdiction over the public two-year institutions. As of summer, 1969, 12 states totally administered these institutions through some agency of the state, 28 did it through a combination of state and local control, and 9 states placed the colleges under the jurisdiction of a university. The few states appearing in two categories reflect dual arrangements.

FULL STATE CONTROL The number of states exercising full control has increased substantially in the last decade. In Colorado, Massachusetts, and Minnesota, among others, local boards recently have relinquished full control to the state or were in the process of doing so. In other states, such as Alabama, Connecticut, Virginia, and Rhode Island, initial legislation for community colleges provided for this type of control at the outset. In states which changed their form of control, the action was taken because the voters in many metropolitan and suburban communities which badly needed community colleges were reluctant to levy taxes for the necessary partial support. While the states making this change have generally given existing community colleges the option of either joining the state system or remaining under a local board, in most instances the institutions have either affiliated with the state plan or have taken steps to do so.

As indicated in Table 19, the governing board for fully state-controlled community colleges is either separately organized for that purpose or is also responsible for other institutions of higher education in the state. For example, Minnesota's community colleges fall under the jurisdiction of the junior college board, whereas in Georgia the two-year institutions are part of the state's higher education administered through the board of regents of the university system.

Divided Responsibility The practice of operating community colleges under the jurisdiction of a local board but almost always with a degree of control and coordination by the state is the oldest, most prevalent, and most complex of the various governance forms. Its complexity arises out of two situations. The first is the sheer number of separate local governing bodies in states with numerous community colleges. This results in variations in policies and practices throughout the state. Normally the members of local boards are elected by the voters in the legally constituted districts. In a few instances they are appointed by the governor.

Presumably, a separate governing board primarily responsible for the college in a community tends to ensure that the college will be responsive to community needs and characteristics. This contention is difficult to prove, however, and Peterson (1969) has raised questions as to its validity. It may be that the virtues of local control lie as much with the emotional involvement of people and their pride of "ownership" as with the ability of a local board to perceive educational needs.

The second problem is the potential conflict between whatever plan for coordination is built into the state system and the ideal of local control. Almost without exception systems of local control and support are linked with state aid. Even when community colleges were appendages of local public school systems, the state normally contributed part of their operational costs, thus subjecting the colleges to the same elements of state regulation that governed elementary and secondary schools. Now that community colleges are rapidly assuming a prominent place in postsecondary education, a state, as a whole, has even greater interest in their development and efficient operation, hence it increases its scrutiny of them.

Various types of control agencies at the state level have evolved.

	States in which two-year colleges are fully controlled (not including situations in which the institutions are under the general jurisdiction of a state university)	

TABLE 19
Patterns of control for public community colleges, 1969[a]

Under a separate board for community colleges as the principal governing body	Under a board responsible for other higher institutions, although with a subunit primarily responsible for community colleges	With the state's function performed by the state board of education and/or the department of public instruction
Alabama	Georgia	Florida[b]
Colorado[h]	Oklahoma[c]	Idaho
Connecticut	Rhode Island	Iowa
Delaware	Tennessee[d,f]	Kansas
Massachusetts	West Virginia	Michigan[b]
Minnesota		Mississippi[b]
Virginia		Missouri
		Montana
		Nebraska[d]
		Nevada
		North Carolina
		North Dakota
		Oregon
		Pennsylvania[b,c]
		Wisconsin[g]

[a] Exclusive of: Vocational-technical institutions in Connecticut, Maine, New Hampshire, South Carolina, and Vermont; Canal Zone, where college is under military governor; South Dakota, which has no community colleges.
[b] State community college council is advisory to the state department of education through division of community college council.
[c] Community colleges in two control categories.

Referring again to Table 19, it can be observed that some organizational arrangement within the state department of education or public instruction is still the most prevalent means of implementing the state's role in coordinating community colleges. In most states a subunit within these agencies is responsible for community colleges, and these units are becoming increasingly more powerful and sophisticated. There is a recent trend toward either creating separate community college boards or placing the community colleges under a general board which administers other higher institutions. This arrangement presently exists in 12 states. Many community college administrators, as well as local board members,

States in which two-year colleges are controlled
by both local communities and the state

With the state's function performed by a separate board for community colleges	With the state's function performed by a board responsible for other higher institutions	States in which two-year institutions are under the general jurisdiction of one or more state universities
Arizona	Arkansas	Alaska
California	Louisiana ^{c}	Hawaii
Illinois	New Jersey	Indiana ^{e}
Maryland	New York	Kentucky
Washington	Ohio	Louisiana ^{c}
Wyoming	Oklahoma ^{c}	New Mexico
	Texas	Pennsylvania ^{c}
		South Carolina
		Utah
		Wisconsin ^{g}

^{d}Dual boards, one for vocational-technical education.
^{e}Indiana has one locally controlled community college, Vincennes University.
^{f}State department of education.
^{g}Adult and vocational schools under state board for vocational education.
^{h}Local control optional.
SOURCE: Compiled by authors from data from various sources.

regard it as a threat to local autonomy. More relevant, however, is a division of powers and duties between local and state agencies in a manner that will leave to each community college the opportunity to plan and administer its own educational program. A proper division of responsibilities should ensure that community college education for an entire state would accomplish as economically and efficiently as possible what the people, through legislative bodies, have assigned to it. The task of building and managing a "system" of community colleges in a given state can no longer be left to chance, and it may be that no one type of state agency is necessarily superior to another in this regard. Perhaps the current diversity of plans may, in the long run, reveal the most effective organizational pattern.

It seems certain that the trend is in the direction of greater state control over all public higher education, and while there are legitimate concerns as to whether this trend will impinge on the concept of the community college, there are still ways in which a college can maintain a close relationship with its community. Where there is full state control, strong local advisory committees with responsibility for making recommendations to both the college and state board, and the involvement of college administrators and faculty in state planning and policy making, have helped to retain local initiative.

An important aspect of community college development lies in the extent to which there are well-designed state plans for it. In states where these colleges have grown the most, there have been carefully outlined plans for their development. Thus plans are either for community colleges as a separate segment or as parts of master plans for all higher education. A study by Hurlburt (1969) found master planning for higher education a prime concern of state and community leaders. Acknowledging a decade of phenomenal growth in the number of public community colleges throughout the nation, respondents pointed to the increased need for statewide coordination of all units of higher education. Significant purposes of such planning included finding a rational means for establishing support priorities and the efficient allocation of responsibilities among units of higher education.

At least half the states in the nation reported statewide planning in process. Nineteen states had either officially adopted state master plans or had the development of a master plan firmly under way.

Internal Patterns of Governance In the last few years, many people have expressed concern about the available quality and quantity of administrative manpower to enable community colleges to discharge their obligations. Moreover, as have other educational institutions, the community colleges have recently had to face new questions about the decision-making process and the involvement of faculty and students in that process.

As might be expected, community colleges—and for that matter independent two-year colleges—encounter problems concerning a functional organization plan. The common pattern is for a chief administrative officer to be assisted by administrators responsible for student personnel, instructional affairs, and operational affairs. In recent years, additional administrators often have been added to the staff to discharge responsibilities for such tasks as institutional research, campus planning and development, and relationships with outside agencies. Unfortunately, since colleges are organized along divisional lines, smaller departmental units, or both, there is no common model for planning and implementing instructional programs.

During the last decade, there has been rapid development of community college districts which maintain two or more campuses or colleges under one governing board and a central administration. Especially prevalent in large cities where as many as eight campuses may be found, this arrangement also exists in dozens of suburban communities and even in certain rural areas.

Organizational and administrative problems arise in such districts over questions pertaining to centralization and autonomy. Administrators, members of governing boards, and faculty members increasingly seek a model that will give each campus or college freedom to plan and operate in a manner that meets the peculiar needs of its own service area and, at the same time, preserve such advantages as a sufficient tax base to equalize resources among campuses, the possibility of coordinating the educational program for the district, and the achievement of economies from centralized services. The trend is toward giving greater campus autonomy, but the stresses and strains of conflict and tension are ever present.

The historical affiliation of community colleges with public schools, until recently at least, tended to result in a more conservative and conventional approach to governance than that generally found in colleges and universities. Now that their identification is primarily with higher education, however, the traditional hierarchy has been modified in many institutions. In its place are structures which give faculty and, even more recently, students a stronger voice in decision making.

This step is not coming easily, however, and it is not yet understood or condoned by many board members, lay citizens, or administrators. But with the advent of faculty senates, strong labor unions, and forms of negotiating councils, the achievement of consensus and cooperation will be increasingly difficult but no less imperative for the community colleges.

FINANCIAL SUPPORT With 739 two-year public institutions in 1968 enrolling approximately 1.8 million full- and part-time students, and with the number of colleges and students increasing each year, the total cost of operating these institutions and constructing facilities for them is understandably of great magnitude.

Considerations pertaining to the financing of these institutions require a brief discussion. First, there is the philosophical stance held by many individuals that the cost of attending a community college should be very low and that tuition should be either non-existent or minimal. Despite the prevailing belief that an institution designed to democratize higher education should eliminate the charges that tend to prevent students of low economic means from attending it, there are few states where at least a small charge is not required by law or at least made optional. A notable exception is California, where all the community colleges are tuition-free to residents of the state. In contrast, a few states require that students pay tuition amounting to as much as one-third of the operating costs of the community college.

Another factor to consider is the inevitable relationship between patterns of control and support. In states which regard the community college totally as a state function, most—if not all—of the revenue for operating and capital outlay purposes is derived from state funds. On the other hand, in those states which share legal responsibility with local governments, financial responsibility is also shared. In reality, then, there is no single pattern for the support of community colleges but rather a variety, depending upon the legal provisions for these institutions in each state.

Questions are frequently raised about the costs of education at a community college compared with those of other types of colleges, particularly four-year institutions. A comparison is difficult, however, because upper-division and graduate-level education tend to be inherently more costly than education at the lower-division level. Thus it is not valid to compare student costs in community colleges with those in four-year colleges or in universities. Because it is difficult to separate out the true cost of lower-division work in four-year institutions, most cost comparisons of community colleges are questionable. Another problem in making comparisons is the tendency for much of the first two years of classroom teaching in four-year colleges, especially universities, to be conducted by ill-paid teaching assistants, whereas community college instruction is conducted by regular faculty members at greater relative cost.

Other difficulties encountered in making cost comparisons are due to the fact that unit costs vary among community colleges. For example, costs are likely to be higher in newer and smaller institutions. Likewise, vocational-technical curricula tend to be more costly than general academic courses, hence community colleges with strong commitments to prepare students for employment may incur high unit costs.

Given these variable factors it is possible that an exact comparison would reveal that costs are not always lower than those in the lower division of four-year units. A more important consideration, however, is whether community colleges offer instructional programs that better meet the needs of many students whom four-year colleges cannot be expected to serve adequately.

A final consideration is student aid. Concern about the availability of funds to enable poor students to remain in school in face of rising costs has increased dramatically in recent years. In no institution is the problem more serious than in the community college, which, by its nature, enrolls so many students from low-income families. The problem is accentuated as an increasing number of young people from ethnic minority groups aspire to extend their education. Serious doubts can be raised about the viability of the community college as a democratizing agent unless means can be found to assist needy students to take advantage of it.

The foregoing list of questions and problems concerning the financial support of community colleges suggests the complexity of the overall problem and calls attention to some of the reasons why those who advocate and plan for community colleges must be concerned as much about the philosophy of how these institutions are to be supported as with the sources and nature of the support. First of all, it is unwise to consider the community college as a financial bargain, since the cost of educating a student in the first two years of postsecondary education is not necessarily less than in other institutions. A system of community colleges may prove to be economical to a state in that the facilities of the four-year institutions can be utilized to greater advantage for upper-division and graduate students—an important factor in state educational planning. But the community college should not be sold as a "cheap" institution. It is of nominal cost to individual students, and it is economical to society in general because it provides an opportunity for students to live at home.

It is also clear that in considering methods of financing, account must be taken of a fundamental purpose of the community college, namely, its role in equalizing educational opportunity. Elsewhere in this volume, the point is made that enhancing the opportunity for Americans to continue their education beyond high school depends on the proximity of open-door educational institutions and the availability of relevant programs for a diverse student body. But neither the institutions nor the programs can serve students who cannot afford to avail themselves of the opportunities at hand. Hence a third element must be added, namely, financial ease in attendance.

SOURCES AND EXPENDITURES OF FUNDS

An overall picture of the sources of support for community college operations can be obtained from the data in Table 20. It should be noted that for 1965–66 local and state government each contributed approximately one-third of the revenues, and only 13 percent came from tuition and fees. Since these are national figures, they do not represent the situation in any given state inasmuch as this depends in large measure on how a community college system is structured and governed. Where the system is under the full control of a state, a local community is rarely required to contribute substantially toward the support of its college, but where legal responsibility is shared, costs also tend to be widely shared.

Arney (1969), in his study of financial support of community colleges, documents the great variation in support practices that might be expected as a result of varying state plans. His findings with respect to the percent of current expenses derived from the several sources are reported in Table 21. It should be pointed out that Arney's study was confined to the 42 states in which the junior colleges in operation in 1967–68 were, according to his criteria, "comprehensive enough in course offerings to approach the philosophical assumptions espoused by community college leaders." The percentage figures used by Arney were reported by appropriate officials in each state for the year 1967–68. Presumably, the contribution by the federal government in each case was to support special programs, primarily of a vocation-technical nature. The great variation in the percent of expenditures met from this source reflects the nature and size of the total program in each state. Thus, in instances in which the program is vocationally oriented and perhaps of modest size, the percentage of federal funds would be greater than in states with large and more comprehensive programs.

TABLE 20
Revenues,
1965–66—
public two-year
colleges (in
thousands)

Source	Amount*	Percent*
Local government	$236,773	33
State government	241,367	34
Federal government	29,735	4
Tuition and fees	93,547	13
Room, board, and all other charges	43,710	6
Earnings from endowment investments	1,163	1
Private gifts and grants	2,657	3
Other sources	46,483	6
TOTAL	$695,435	100

*Dollar amounts and percentages have been collapsed and rounded.

SOURCE: U.S. Office of Education, National Center for Education Statistics: Adapted from "Financial Statistics of Institutions of Higher Education," *Current Funds and Revenue Expenditures 1965–66,* Washington, D.C., 1969.

Attention is called to the 27 states (designated in Table 21 by an asterisk) which share control and support with the local community. While the proportion borne by either the state or the local agency may be expected to vary because of tuition and other factors, it is noteworthy that state and local partnership in support of current expenses is the predominant pattern. Here, Arney's data indicate a significant shift in this decade to a more equitable sharing of current expenses between local and state agencies. Citing as a basis for comparison the study of Morrison and Martorana (1962), Arney reports that the median state support for current expenses increased by 10 percent, from 26 (1960–61) to 36 percent (1967–68). Conversely, median local support decreased by 10 percent, from 40 (1960–61) to 30 percent (1967–68). Thus, the sharing of approximately one-third each of the current revenues by local and state agencies reflects the national view of support for community college operations, as shown in Table 20, and indicates the growing acceptance by state agencies of financial responsibility for community college development.

The extent to which proportions of support borne by the various sources will vary from year to year is partly a function of the mechanism for determining revenue. Arney discovered that in the 42 states in his study, state funds were allocated by an objective formula in 25 instances. In 17 states the funds were made by legislative appropriations. Of the 25 states using an objective formula, only three—California, Florida, and Montana—combined the formula with equalization features. In any case, it is inevitable that the

TABLE 21 *Percent of current expenses for the budget year 1967–68, as reported by state officials, by source*

State	Federal	State	Local supporting district	Local charge-back	Student fees and tuition	Other
Alabama	21	59	0	0	18	2
*Arizona	3	47	43	6	1	0
*Arkansas	10	32	31	0	25	2
*California	3	32	60	1	0	4
Colorado	2	40	31	0	15	12
Connecticut	1	79	0	0	20[a]	0
Delaware	0	100	0	0	0	0
*Florida	5	59	11	0	24	1
Georgia[b]	4	69	0	0	25	2
Hawaii	23	75	0	0	2	0
*Idaho	2	40	27	5	24	1
*Illinois	2	31	47	6	12	2
Indiana	10	13	2	0	31	44
*Iowa	12	55	17	0	14	2
*Kansas	5	17	40	21	14	3
Kentucky	2	98	0	0	0	0
*Louisiana	24	59	0	0	8	9
*Maryland	6	21	47	1	25	0
Massachusetts	4	71	0	0	25[a]	0
*Michigan	2	36	26	0	29	7
Minnesota	2	71	0	0	27	0
*Mississippi	11	39	35	2	11	2
*Missouri	5	31	37	0	17	10
*Montana	4	59	20	0	17	0
*Nebraska	0	26	35	0	33	6
*Nevada	0	4	0	0	34	62
*New Jersey	0	50	25	0	25	0
New Mexico	11	0	33	0	51	5
*New York	2	32	38	5	21	2
*North Carolina	2	79	11	0	8	0
*North Dakota[c]	8	42	20	0	29	1
North Dakota[d]	0	67	0	0	33	0
*Ohio	2	36	25	0	30	7
*Oklahoma	0	59	4	0	32	5

State	Federal	State	Local supporting district	Local charge-back	Student fees and tuition	Other
*Oregon	7	48	22	0	23	0
*Pennsylvania	7	31	31	0	23	0
Rhode Island	1	63	0	0	18	18
Tennessee	15	62	0	0	13	10
*Texas	0	51	30	0	19	0
Utah	8	67	0	0	13	1
Virginia	10	79	0	0	11	0
*Washington	11	76	0	0	13	0
*Wyoming	4	31	43	0	17	5

*States in which control and support are shared with the local community.
[a] Student fees and tuition go into the state general fund from which total operating expenses are funded.
[b] Excludes one locally controlled college.
[c] For locally controlled colleges.
[d] For state-controlled colleges.

SOURCE: L. H. Arney, "A Comparison of Patterns of Financial Support with Selected Criteria in Community Junior Colleges," unpublished doctoral dissertation, University of Florida, 1969.

proportion by source will vary over time and that conditions will arise which necessitate a change in adopted formulas. This is clearly seen in the case of the community college system in New York, where the support formula originally specifically allocated a third of the operating costs each to the state, to the local sponsoring agency, and to the students. The formula ran into difficulty because, as unit costs increased, the one-third contributed by students in the form of tuition and fees became excessive. The formula now provides that the state will bear up to 40 percent of the operating costs. Students may be charged tuition up to $400 per year. The local sponsoring agency then makes up the difference between the amount contributed by the state and paid by the students. The local agency may if it chooses charge a smaller tuition.

Expenditures for Operation Of general interest is the manner in which revenues are distributed among categories of expenditures. As a supplement to the information in Table 20, the expenditures for 1965–66 in public two-year institutions are reported in Table 22. The substantial percentage of the income that was expended for instructional and related purposes tends to document the fundamental characteristics of the community college as a teaching institution.

TABLE 22
*Expenditures,
1965–66—
public two-year
colleges (in
thousands)*

Category	Amount*	Percent*
Instructional	$340,835	52
Extension and public service	19,015	3
Libraries	22,358	4
Physical plant maintenance	61,879	10
General administration	88,566	11
Other educational and general	23,981	4
Student aids and grants	5,169	1
Auxiliary enterprises	52,548	9
Current funds for physical assets	38,106	6
TOTAL	$652,456	100

*Dollar amounts and percentages have been collapsed and rounded.

SOURCE: Adapted from the U.S. Office of Education, National Center for Education Statistics: "Financial Statistics of Institutions of Higher Education," *Current Funds and Revenue Expenditures 1965–66,* Washington, D.C., 1969.

**Funds for
Capital Outlay**

Arney (1969) also solicited information from state agencies concerning the sources of funds for capital outlay. The information he obtained for 1967–68, which is reported in Table 23, again clearly depicts the diversity of practices among states.

The rather heavy contribution by the federal government reflects the impact of the Higher Education Facilities Act of 1963 and subsequent amendments which authorized that a substantial percentage of the funds be designated for community colleges on a matching basis by state and local agencies. Despite the gap between authorizations and appropriations during the intervening years, the community colleges have been assisted materially although perhaps unevenly. Furthermore, federal contributions for any given year in a given state may be very different from other years, not only because of the variation in federal funds available but also because the eligibility of the community colleges in the state to receive funds varies from year to year.

Many of the states have a formula for the sharing of state and local efforts for capital outlay. In New York, for example, the capital costs are shared equally by the state and local community, and this formula has been adopted in a number of other states. In Illinois, the current formula calls for a state contribution of 75 percent, with the local district responsible for the remaining 25 percent. The receipt of federal funds reduces the percentage charged to the state and the local community. Other states have specific provisions unrelated to a percentage factor. For example, Arizona provides $115 annually per full-time student equivalent and $500 per campus, with the remainder of the funds coming from the local county. Still other states operate on a more current basis and are dependent upon legislative appropriations and the revenue from periodic bond issues to assist local communities. In a number of states where community colleges are under local control, no limit is set on the funds that may be raised locally for building purposes.

The diversity in practice and policy accounts for the great variation in the percentage of funds from each source reported in Table 23. Obviously the burden borne by the local community in states in which the community college is entirely a state function is either zero or very small. But in those states, designated in Table 23 by an asterisk, where the state and local community share the responsibility, there is no common pattern.

ISSUES WITH REGARD TO SUPPORT It would be easy to assert that the overriding concern about the support of the community college is whether it can be adequately financed. But this is a concern about *all* educational units from kindergarten through the university, and perhaps some degree of faith must be placed in the ultimate will of society to support its schools and colleges. On the other hand, there is evidence that local school districts as well as legislatures are showing signs of resistance to increased taxes, so the matter cannot be taken lightly.

Here again, the discussion must start by recognizing the close relationship between control and support. As previously indicated, the two prevalent forms of control are the fully state-controlled plan and the sharing of control between the state and local community. It is easy to advance financial arguments in favor of either plan. It can be said, for example, that a state plan ensures more uniform support and that it does so from a statewide tax base, rather than in part from a local base that is often the victim of antiquated tax practices. Proponents of the combination of state and local effort, in addition to pointing to philosophical reasons why a *community* college should be partly a product of its immediate environment, claim that it can tap local resources and willing support in excess of all possibilities from state effort alone. There is no simple response to either argument, and certainly there is no major reason why either plan should be abandoned in favor of the other. One point that *is* clear, however, is the necessity that in states which share the responsibility the contribution must be substantial, so that the local community is not burdened with an inordinate part of the cost of either operation or capital outlay.

TABLE 23 *Percent of capital outlay for the budget year 1967–68, as reported by state officials, by source*

State	Federal	State	Local supporting district	Local charge-back	Student fees and tuition	Other
Alabama	90	10	0	0	0	0
*Arizona	8	78	14	0	0	0
*Arkansas	32	8	60	0	0	0
*California	6	17	77	0	0	0
Colorado	40	30	30	0	0	0
Connecticut	a	a	0	0	0	0
Delaware	11	78	0	0	11	0
*Florida	4	90	4	0	0	2
Georgia	24	50	0	0	0	26
Hawaii	7	93	0	0	0	0
*Idaho	59	1	30	0	0	10
*Illinois	0	75	25	0	0	0
Indiana	44	27	0	0	0	29
*Iowa	8	51	39	0	0	2
*Kansas	23	77	0	0	0	0
Kentucky[b]	62	38	0	0	0	0
*Louisiana[c]						
*Maryland	3	47	50	0	0	0
Massachusetts	18	82	0	0	0	0
*Michigan	20	21	59	0	0	0
Minnesota	a	a	0	0	0	0
*Mississippi	45	38	17	0	0	0
*Missouri	12	2	86	0	0	0
*Montana	0	0	100	0	0	0
*Nebraska	0	0	100	0	0	0
*Nevada[c]						
*New Jersey	12	44	44	0	0	0
New Mexico	88	0	12	0	0	0
*New York	23	38	38	d	0	0
*North Carolina	32	18	50	0	0	0
*North Dakota	40	0	60	0	0	0
*Ohio[d]						
*Oklahoma	25	62	13	0	0	0
*Oregon[e]	21	43	36	0	0	0

State	Federal	State	Local supporting district	Local charge-back	Student fees and tuition	Other
*Pennsylvania	0	50	50	0	0	0
Rhode Island	100	0	0	0	0	0
Tennessee	40	60	0	0	0	0
*Texas	a	0	a	0	0	0
Utah	a	a	0	0	0	0
Virginia[f]	37	39	24	0	0	0
*Washington[d]						
*Wyoming	25	8	61	0	0	6

*States in which control and support are shared with the local community.
[a] Exact amount unavailable.
[b] Student tuition is pledged for bonds for capital outlay.
[c] No capital outlay in 1967–1968.
[d] Information unavailable.
[e] Based on completed construction from 1962–1968.
[f] Based on 1966–1968 biennium.
SOURCE: L. H. Arney, "A Comparison of Patterns of Financial Support with Selected Criteria in Community Junior Colleges," unpublished doctoral dissertation, University of Florida, 1969.

The responsibility of the federal government is of increasing concern. Proposed legislation, particularly that introduced by Senator Harrison Williams, and in the 91st session of Congress, recognizes the necessity for greater financial assistance from federal sources if the community college is to make the forward leap which public opinion seems to dictate. It seems reasonable to predict that with the recognized need for additional community colleges and further development of those already in existence, additional federal assistance must and will increase. Questions will be raised as to whether community colleges should be distinguished from other segments of education for special help. The response must naturally be based in part on the acuteness of the problem which the nation faces in extending postsecondary education, particularly to such groups as the urban poor, who to date have been underrepresented in higher education.

A still completely unresolved issue is the one of tuition. Arney (1969) reported that in 1968 only three of the 42 states in his study had laws which prohibited tuition in the community colleges, whereas 29 of the states permitted tuition, and 19 required it. The percentage of operating costs supported by tuition and fees as reported in Table 21 ranges all the way from 0 to 51, with the median about 20 percent. It is important to note that data in this study indicate a trend toward lower tuition, in keeping with the democratized role of the public community college. In reference again to the Martorana and Morrison support survey, Arney reports a notable decrease in the median percent of tuition contribution for current expenses. For the fully state-controlled community college systems, the median tuition was 24 percent in 1960–61, but only 18 percent in 1967–68 — a drop of 6 percent. For the same period, the median student support for operating expenses of community college systems with shared state-local responsibilities decreased 8 percent, from 32 in 1960–61 to 24 percent in 1967–68.

Arney concludes that in this decade "the percent of increase in federal support for community junior colleges, and the percent of increase in state support for operation of locally controlled junior colleges . . . offset the percent of increase of college operating expenses paid by the student." This reported trend, as significant as it may first appear, should be understood perhaps as only a modest anticipation of the time when postsecondary public education — at least at the community college level — can be offered at minimal cost to American citizens. And the question, within the larger issue of the future of institutional support, of how America's urban poor and disadvantaged minorities are to pay even the minimal costs of postsecondary education is still unanswered. Because of this the Carnegie Commission recommended that states revise their legislation, whenever necessary, to provide for uniform low tuition charges at public two-year institutions.

Still another remaining issue pertains to the availability of funds for student assistance, which is more pressing in community colleges than in most other types of institutions. Because of legal restrictions which prohibit funds from local tax sources from being made available directly to individuals, legislation to liberalize the use of tax funds may prove necessary. In addition, implementation of one of several proposed plans (including one by the Carnegie Commission, June, 1970, App. B) emphasizing federal aid to students is needed for higher education generally and specifically for the community college.

Serious thought must be given to the mounting overall cost of community colleges in the next decade. Those who might view critically the outlay of funds necessary to maintain a national network of community colleges should keep in mind two fundamental points. First, total expenditures for *all* higher education will inevitably increase. Whether it is less costly to educate lower-division students in community colleges than in four-year colleges is not clear. Nonetheless, an efficient use of faculty and facilities at *all* levels of higher education may depend upon the ability of the community colleges to absorb a large proportion of lower-division students.

The second and more important point is that the nation's needs are such that the services of the comprehensive community colleges are required for functions not fulfilled by other types of institutions. Accordingly, the intrinsic value of community colleges must justify their costs. It could be argued that the community college increases the total cost of higher education because it attracts into the college stream—even the baccalaureate stream—students who otherwise would never consider college. But this argument has to be considered in terms of the economic and social advantages—to the individual and to society—of an increase in the general education level of the population.

8. The Independent Junior College

Both two- and four-year private colleges are often the concern of state studies, journal articles, and reported research findings documenting their growing plight. While such attention is often focused upon prestigious institutions such as Harvard and Yale, the problems are found as frequently, and often more so, at the junior colleges, many of which are small and relatively poorly supported.

Representatives of nonpublic two-year colleges prefer the term *independent,* and this term is generally used here, although the phrase *private junior college* appears occasionally to facilitate public understanding. Within the broad classification of independent junior colleges are various subcategories. Although terminology varies, common practice is to refer to *nonsectarian* and *church-related,* with the latter divided between Protestant and Catholic.

Data reported in Chapter 2 reveal that, over the years, enrollment in independent colleges has tended to decrease but may now be stabilizing. In 1968 there were 143,152 students in 254 colleges. It is worth noting, however, that between 1967 and 1968, 10 independent colleges ceased operations and seven others became four-year institutions. The data on page 126, adapted from the 1969 *Directory* of the American Association of Junior Colleges, indicated that the majority of these colleges and students were concentrated in the central, southern, and eastern regions of the nation with only a handful in the western region. Sixty percent of the institutions listed were church-related; 68 of these were Roman Catholic, 25 Baptist, 20 Methodist, and 56 from other Protestant groups.

In general, most independent colleges are small. Only 34 reported in the 1969 *Directory* enrollments in excess of 1,000 students. Half of them were in the 500 to 1,000 category, and 47 reported a student body of less than 100.

Region	Number of colleges	Enrollment
Western	4	913
Northwest	6	5,682
North Central	62	27,169
Southern	80	40,525
Middle States	66	37,075
New England	36	31,788
TOTAL	254	143,152

NATURE OF THE INDEPENDENT COLLEGES

The extreme diversity among the independent colleges precludes an accurate description of them. They vary tremendously in purpose, student body characteristics, offerings, and costs.

Student characteristics

In 1968 slightly more than 100 of the institutions were non-coeducational—74 of them for women and 28 for men.[1] Because of the varying degree to which the independent colleges are selective, it is not surprising to find a wide range of student ability and prior performance levels. This is also true of family background and socioeconomic characteristics, despite the high cost of attending most independent colleges.

In Chapter 3 are reported many data on the characteristics of students attending both public and independent two-year colleges. Comparisons are made of the student bodies in the two types of institutions. In general, the data show that students in independent, nondenominational colleges are quite similar in intellectual predispositions and academic ability to students in public colleges. Church-related colleges, however, are somewhat more selective in terms of academic ability than either nondenominational or public colleges.

[1] This statistic and certain other data reported in this chapter came from a study conducted under the auspices of the American Association of Junior Colleges and supported by a grant from the Alfred P. Sloan Foundation which was reported by Kenneth C. MacKay in spring, 1969. The project was designed to identify "the concerns, problems, issues, needs, and plans of the non-public two-year colleges." More than 250 such institutions responded to a questionnaire form which solicited information and opinions about a variety of matters. The authors of this profile gratefully acknowledge the assistance given them by the report and the opportunity to participate in certain discussions of the findings.

Not only do the characteristics of students in independent colleges vary greatly from institution to institution; it is also possible that differences exist from region to region. In fact, Darley (1962), in his report of an earlier study of entering students in a sample of 200 randomly selected higher institutions in the United States, commented:

The best public institution in the north-central area draws the same level of ability as the best private institutions in the northeast area, among the same level of schools. In the southern region, one public institution is more selective than all Protestant institutions, although the schools of this level in this area are less selective than similar schools in the other three regions.

Obviously, there is "more than meets the eye" in any review of who attends an independent college, and quantitative data can be used only as a general guideline. Undoubtedly, a variety of personal factors account for decisions to enter independent colleges. Many students presumably go to church-related colleges because they or their parents feel the necessity for such an influence. Some may seek the smaller two-year college as an escape from the largeness and perceived impersonality of the public institutions or even the larger, private, four-year colleges. It may also be assumed that many who aspire to "go away to college" are not admissible to the four-year college of their choice, but are able to enter a two-year independent college. Whatever the motives, they constitute important factors for these colleges to consider as they plan educational programs for their clientele.

Educational programs
No attempt is made here to describe in detail the curriculum of the two-year independent college. Again, diversity would make this impossible. For the most part, these colleges stress the transfer function, although nearly all of them also provide a number of occupationally oriented curricula, usually at the semiprofessional level. A few are technical institutes and others are military institutes. By reason of the types of students enrolled, many have to be concerned with remedial work.

Some idea of how the representatives of the independent colleges view their responsibilities is gained by the way they responded to a question in the AAJC study regarding the "real and distinct advantages of the private two-year college." The greatest emphasis is placed on individual attention to students, particularly through small student-teacher ratios, extra help, individual instruction, and counseling. Next in order of emphasis was a category of "freedom-autonomy" which stressed the ability of the private college to adapt to new situations, to innovate, to exercise independence, and to remain free of political pressure. Ranking third was the role of this type of institution in providing an interim college experience, and in fourth place was the perceived advantage of a residential college. The report itself stresses the unique role of personalizing education, of emphasizing the individual, and of serving the underachiever. The respondents also stress innovation and list a number of programs and activities which they claim are neither intended as inclusive nor as necessarily successful. These programs and the colleges which report them are described in the report under the following categories: community projects, international projects, in-service training, cooperation with other educational institutions, inner-city projects for disadvantaged individuals, and "others." Some 40 colleges report projects, although several are credited with two or more programs which are considered innovative.

From the literature, and also from a survey of college catalogs, it may be concluded that a number of the independent colleges are exercising initiative in meeting some of today's educational problems. On the other hand, serious questions can be raised about the ability of many of the very small institutions, or those that face grave financial problems, to offer an enriched program of education or services.

Cost of attendance

Although the financial problems of the independent junior college are discussed subsequently, the charges which, by necessity, it imposes on its students are among its obvious characteristics. Here again, a wide range is found. As a group, the nonsectarian colleges are much more costly than church-related ones inasmuch as many of them attract students from high-socioeconomic-level homes, provide better than average facilities, and offer a wide range of educational, cultural, and recreational programs. The analysis of cost data in Table 24 was derived from figures reported in the 1969 *Directory* of the American Association of Junior Colleges.

By noting the median tuition and the median charges for board

TABLE 24 Cost of attending private junior colleges		Independent nonpublic		Roman Catholic		Protestant	
		Tuition	Room and board	Tuition	Room and board	Tuition	Room and board
	Highest	3,300	2,050	1,500	1,760	3,300	1,210
	Median	1,110	1,025	685	700	650	650
	Lowest	340	350	15	150	117	255

SOURCE: 1969 *Directory*, American Association of Junior Colleges.

and room for each of the three types of independent colleges, it can be concluded that even in the church-related colleges total costs are well beyond those that many potential students can meet. Moreover, with the tendency for these charges to be increased each year, it could be assumed that the colleges might soon price themselves out of the market; this is certainly one of the more significant problems confronting them.

PROBLEMS FACED BY INDEPENDENT COLLEGES In the AAJC study, representatives of the independent colleges were asked, "What are the chief issues or problems facing your college now?" The three most frequently designated were, in this order, financing, staffing, and student recruitment.

Financial problems

The financial plight of private educational institutions needs no documentation here. Suffice it to say that the situation is probably more serious in most of the two-year colleges than in many of the four-year institutions. Most of the two-year colleges have relatively small endowments and as a group receive only modest gifts; thus they are highly dependent upon tuition and other types of current income, as depicted vividly in Chart 12. The fact that over 60 percent of the income from some 180 two-year colleges came from tuition places them in a vulnerable position in a period of inflation. Data taken from the National Center for Education Statistics show that the average expenditure per student in all private two-year institutions in 1965–66 was $868 — more than $300 in excess of the average for public two-year institutions. Essentially the same story is told in Tables 25 and 26, in which total revenue and expenditures for all independent two-year institutions are reported for 1965–66.

TABLE 25
Revenues,
1965–66 —
private
two-year
colleges
(in thousands)

Source	Amount*	Percent*
Local government	$ 0	0
State	528	1
Federal	4,049	2
Tuition and fees	92,720	52
Room, board and all other charges	50,170	28
Earnings from endowment investments	3,784	2
Private gifts and grants	20,232	11
Other sources	7,113	4
TOTAL	$178,596	100

*Dollar amounts and percentages have been collapsed and rounded.
SOURCE: Adapted from U. S. Office of Education, National Center for Education Statistics: "Financial Statistics of Institutions of Higher Education," *Current Funds and Revenue Expenditures 1965–66,* Washington, D.C., 1969.

The situation in which the independent junior colleges find themselves is aptly described in the following statement appearing in the AAJC report:

The responses show that many of the colleges are groping in the dark about their financial problems, too small to muster an effective alumni appeal, too limited to employ a full-time development director, and unable or unwilling to make long-term commitments. They are sensitive to the fact that corporate and foundation philanthropy has passed them by. Many of them

TABLE 26
Expenditures,
1965–66 —
private
two-year
colleges
(in thousands)

Source	Amount*	Percent*
Instructional	$ 50,641	32
Extension and public service	1,402	1
Libraries	4,808	3
Physical plant maintenance	17,120	12
General administration	35,236	20
Other educational and general	6,069	3
Student aid grants	4,069	2
Auxiliary enterprises	40,127	23
Current funds for physical assets	7,204	4
TOTAL	$166,676	100

*Dollar amounts and percentages have been collapsed and rounded.
SOURCE: Adapted from U.S. Office of Education, National Center for Education Statistics: "Financial Statistics of Institutions of Higher Education, *Current Funds and Revenue Expenditures 1965–66,* Washington, D.C., 1969.

feel frustrated by the cruel anomaly of academic life that accreditation requires financial stability and that non-accreditation often precludes the financial assistance to assure this necessary stability.

Obviously there is no single, simple solution to this dilemma. Moreover, the financial situation is interwoven with other problems, and possible solutions may lie with a multidimensional approach rather than a piecemeal effort.

Staffing

The correlation between staffing problems and financial restrictions is reflected by the relatively low salaries paid to faculty members in the independent colleges. The National Education Association (1968) reveals that the median salary in independent two-year colleges is approximately $2,000 lower than it is in public two-year institutions. Garrison (1969) makes the statement that "salaries in private two-year colleges range from $1,500 to $4,000 a year *less* than in most two-year colleges, and this gap is widening."

Difficulty in recruiting and retaining competent faculty members was reported as a crucial problem by a large percentage of the presidents in the AAJC survey. To what degree the problem is

CHART 12
Sources of income as reported by 179 private two-year colleges, 1968

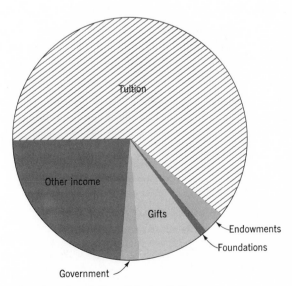

SOURCE: American Association of Junior Colleges.

related to the sheer scarcity of able people who are sufficiently mobile to change their place of residence or to the salary differential is difficult to determine.

Student recruitment

Here again the problem is related to financing because rising student costs not only reduce the gross number of students that can afford independent colleges, but also make ability to pay the principal selection criterion. The result is that the independent colleges face a decline in well-qualified students. Garrison (1969) asserts that whereas 10 or 15 years ago many private colleges had an application acceptance ratio of 3 and 4 to 1, their ratio now is more likely to be 2 to 1, or even less.

Independent college presidents appear to feel, rather keenly, a sense of competition between their type of college and the public community college. They point to the widespread attention given to the latter on almost every front, including within the AAJC, and imply a sort of unplanned but nevertheless effective conspiracy against the private sector. That they would be on the defensive is understandable. On the other hand, the future of the independent two-year college will rest alone on what constructive steps can be taken in its behalf and not at all on any diminishing attention to the public sector.

Naturally, not all the problems faced by the independent two-year college are represented in the categories discussed above. Like all other institutions they are concerned with many additional issues, such as determining their most appropriate administrative and decision-making patterns, planning for the future, and curriculum development. Perhaps the most perplexing problem of all, however, is the lack of a clear-cut image of what the independent college is or should be, an identity that is often missing in the minds of those connected with such a college as well as of the general public.

THE FUTURE It seems evident that with mounting problems the independent colleges face adjustments in the period immediately ahead. The financial crisis must be met in new ways. Further drastic increases in tuition would not only lead to diminishing returns, but would also result in atypical student bodies. Alumni, endowment, and foundation sources cannot generally be counted on for a solution.

Federal aid to students and other types of federal assistance would help. Several states are now considering—and to some extent implementing—plans for state aid to private institutions; these offer new hope for schools that can meet standards.

But more drastic measures are in order. It seems likely that a substantial number of independent two-year colleges will find it necessary to discontinue operations in the near future. These will be, and of course should be, the ones which, because of small size and inherent weaknesses, simply cannot maintain a program worthy of support. Garrison has expressed doubt that more than 60 or 70 will be in existence by 1980. Others have placed the number of survivors at around 150. It is probable that if new means of financing the institutions are to be found, only the best ones will be able to compete for the support.

On the other hand, it is clear that numerous independent colleges are performing an important role and ways should be found to keep them in existence and strengthen them. Their continuation is as important to society as is the continuation of the best independent four-year colleges, and there are not many people who advocate *their* demise.

But in the process of planning for the future, the independent colleges themselves will have to exert influence and leadership. There are signs that this process is well under way. The AAJC study—a study conducted largely by representatives of the independent colleges—is an example of their willingness to examine themselves. In August, 1969, an announcement was made of the formation of a National Council of Independent Two-Year Colleges. The Council, which will work closely with the American Association of Junior Colleges, has set the following goals:

That the colleges represented in the National Council would develop a system of orientation for staff, in-service training, faculty recruitment policies, and cooperative arrangements with selected colleges to identify and develop those particular qualities which contribute to the junior college concept.

That the colleges will exert every effort to become active, essential partners with other segments of their communities in social and civic undertakings.

That the colleges will keep their programs and projects under constant scrutiny in order to sustain an institutional alertness to educational and social needs.

The goals are commendable and should result in strengthening a number of the member institutions.

No future course is certain, but it is clear that time, attention, and support must be directed toward salvaging at least part of a junior college segment that society cannot afford to lose.

9. Summary, Issues, and Recommendations

This profile has been prepared for those who are concerned about the role and scope of the two-year college in American postsecondary education. More specifically, the objectives of the authors were to document the extent and nature of the junior colleges' contributions to society, to identify some of their problems, to comment on their probable future, and to make certain recommendations so that they may more likely fulfill their obligations.

Naturally, it has not been possible to deal in depth with all aspects of a group of institutions that is expanding rapidly and assuming many responsibilities. The objectives have been limited to providing a brief overview, without a detailed analysis, of the junior colleges—including their problems and apparent potential.

INDEPENDENT JUNIOR COLLEGES Although both the number of independent two-year colleges and their enrollments have gradually declined over the last few years, they continue to play an important role, particularly in the central, southern, and eastern regions of the country. In 1968, the more than 250 independent junior colleges enrolled 143,152 students. Both the institutions and their students are exceedingly diverse, and it appears that most of the students electing to attend them are able to find one which meets their individual needs and expectations.

Two problems are of special concern. Many of the independent colleges are so small that questions arise as to their ability to offer an adequate program. In 1968, almost 50 of them had enrollments of fewer than 100 students. Many others were in the 100 to 500 category. Then there is the problem of financial support. Well over half the revenue for independent two-year colleges is derived from tuition and fees. College costs and the ability of families to meet them in an inflationary economy poses serious questions about the future of many private institutions.

Despite these problems, the independent institutions show renewed vigor for sustaining themselves and taking advantage of their unique position in higher education in a period of changing values. While it is likely that the total number of independent colleges will gradually be reduced, it is expected that within a few years the remaining core will consist of those which have seriously examined their purposes and programs and have taken steps to attract students and staff who provide vitality and distinctiveness. Even in these institutions, however, financial problems will remain paramount. Ways must be found to augment student fees as a means of supporting these colleges. They enable many students to benefit from practices unlikely to be found in public community colleges.

PUBLIC COMMUNITY COLLEGES That the public community college is becoming increasingly significant in American higher education is evidenced by its growth and widespread recognition throughout the nation. More than a third of all entering college students now begin their work in a community college. Already for the country as a whole community colleges enroll about 8 percent of the 18- to 24-year-old population; by 1980 this may rise as high as 11 percent. As reported in Chapter 1, their phenomenal development and the projected number of students they may enroll within the next decade identifies them as the fastest-growing segment of American education.

Perhaps it could be said that the sheer growth and recognition of the community college reflect its significance since, if it were not filling perceived needs, it could hardly be expected to increase in size and stature. A review of the demands that are placed on it, and of the services it renders, suggests that it plays two dominant roles. In the first place, it serves an ever-increasing percentage of recent high school graduates who enter it either with the expectation of continuing their education later in a four-year institution or of finding employment after leaving it. In this capacity, the community college is a distributing agency operating between the secondary school on the one hand and various social institutions on the other. As it comes more and more to discharge these functions, it tends to effect a reorganization of American education: for students who at least complete a baccalaureate degree, the pattern of education becomes an 8-4-2-2 arrangement instead of the traditional 8-4-4 pattern. It is noteworthy that the community college, as an added unit in the educational structure, encourages the flow of students from school to college, making it possible for many to achieve certain goals within the two-year period, while still keeping the channels open for further education. Its very presence, together with its demonstrated ability and willingness to serve older youth and adults, enables an unlimited number of individuals to pursue an educational interest at will and thus reopens the door that often closes when a person terminates his formal full-time education.

A delineation of the community college's role is incomplete, however, without reference to its democratization of postsecondary education. Koos (1925) early called attention to this attribute of the junior college, and his observation has since gained support. An open-door policy, proximity to clientele, low cost to students, and a multiplicity of programs all combine to make the community college potentially effective in extending educational opportunity. Applying existing research data against these criteria, Cross (1969) concluded that despite certain inequities among geographical regions, lack of motivation on the part of certain types of students, and certain deficiencies in the range of programs, "there is cause for optimism regarding the capacity and spirit of the two-year colleges in providing postsecondary education for all." Yet, the authors are concerned about the gap between expectations and fulfillment.

ISSUES FACED BY THE COMMUNITY COLLEGE While the community college has made great strides, much still remains to be done. Obviously, the list of grave problems confronting it (or, for that matter, any educational institution) is long. Necessarily, then, a high degree of selectivity must be used to identify the most crucial issues. The following ones seem particularly significant.

Understanding the New Concept If it were necessary to identify the single most significant emerging characteristic of education beyond the high school, most scholars in the field would probably point to its egalitarian nature. To be sure, the idea of equality of opportunity is not new. Nonetheless, over the years quasi-elitist practices have prevailed in American higher education. Two developments in the 1940s were instrumental in effecting a significant change in direction. One of these was the mass enrollment of World War II veterans under the G.I. Bill of Rights; the other was the much-publicized pronouncement by President Truman's Commission on Higher Education that 49 percent of the population had the mental ability to complete 14 years of schooling. Since then, reports by many other agencies and commissions have pointed toward the goal of equalizing opportunity for education beyond the high school. The trend was greatly accelerated by the civil rights movement, and higher education soon will be called upon to accommodate many groups that hitherto have been underrepresented.

Despite the move in this direction, there is no complete understanding of and sympathy for the movement in all segments of society. Peter Schrag (1969) comments on the "end of the bull market in higher education" and specifically notes legislative cuts for programs serving disadvantaged students. The problem ahead was stated forcefully by Logan Wilson (1970) when he said: "Whether without vastly increased public understanding and support educational institutions can meet the demands placed upon them is open to question. About the growing aspirations of the American people, however, there can be no question."

To fully implement the egalitarian principle, there must be a change in the concept of education beyond the high school from that of *higher education,* as it has been known over the centuries, to that of *postsecondary* education, which embraces an array of institutions and programs even more diverse than we have had to date. The community college will be in the forefront of these institutions, but it will be only one of several offering opportunity for nonbaccalaureate study. The problem obviously is not that the community college lacks general acceptance by the nation—its rapid growth to date indicates its popularity—but the serious question is whether, in a period of belt-tightening, it will have sufficient public understanding and support to enable it to serve the increasing number of students who heretofore have not continued their education beyond the secondary school and who will be served best by institutions with unconventional functions and practices.

Implementing the Goal of Equal Opportunity

Some of the rhetoric about universal higher education deludes both policy makers and educators and makes false promises to those who have yet to enter the mainstream of American life. It is particularly threatening to the community college, which is emerging as the target institution to do those things which other colleges and universities cannot or will not do. Unfortunately, it is widely assumed that the community college can succeed in educating great numbers of new students at less cost than other agencies and that it will have the personnel and freedom from tradition to do the job. But in the nation there is neither the planning nor the commitment to provide universal higher education in the foreseeable future. Progress is being made in broadening participation in postsecondary education, and junior colleges have from their beginning been on the cutting edge in this move. Their metamorphosis into a comprehensive community institution gives increased hope for educating new groups of students beyond high school. Even so, many barriers still exist.

But equal opportunity and wide participation in higher education involve more than merely lowering the barriers to admission. There is ample evidence, for example, that postsecondary education is not meeting the needs of many students, particularly those who are below the median in financial resources, in traditional measures of academic ability and school achievement, and in interests and values usually cherished in American colleges. How can the junior colleges invite students to enter their open doors unless they have the needed programs and services? The challenge to be relevant seems to have been accepted, but new talents, new resources, and new programs are necessary.

Barriers to admission. The availability of low-cost and relevant postsecondary education is still a national problem. Some students are deprived of opportunity because of where they live, their racial and ethnic backgrounds, their financial resources, and because of nonacademic interests and school histories. And even though barriers are being systematically lowered through widespread development of two-year colleges and through changing concepts of financial aid, large sections of the country (particularly the Eastern seaboard and the South) lack adequate low-cost comprehensive institutions. There are a few states which recognize in their financial aid programs the importance of forgone earnings to the decisions of sons and daughters of the poor to go to college or not. Not only do heavy work schedules, family indebtedness, and economic pressures contribute to the vulnerability of many who enter junior colleges, but many young people under such pressures choose not to try college at all. Low tuition, then, is not enough to remove the economic barriers to education.

The continued emphasis on traditional academic critieria in preparing students for college discourages young people with nonacademic talents and interests. Such practices are reinforced by college admission requirements, and together they result in restricted opportunity for the children of the poor and minority groups. Negative attitudes toward vocational education and the lack of programs for career development are by-products of the academic syndrome in American higher education.

The revolving door. Perhaps one-third of the students who enter junior colleges find themselves in limbo and are soon on their way out—dismissed for low achievement in programs they could not handle, turned off by instruction which is irrelevant to their interests, or overwhelmed by financial pressures. It is likely that many of these students find no hospitable place, either in the high-status transfer program or in the highly selective technical and semiprofessional curricula of the contemporary community college. This gap in program comprehensiveness, when combined with deficiencies in guidance and developmental education, means that many students find no programs which offer opportunities for them.

Maintaining a Comprehensive Program In view of evidence that the community college is an emerging institution with a considerable gap between promise and practice, the adequacy of its program becomes an issue of central concern.

There is no single model nor any compelling theory or body of research to use in defining and assessing comprehensiveness. However, the problems of scope, integration, organization, and commitment are important issues in determining the adequacy of the community college program.

Scope of program. Community colleges differ markedly in the breadth of their curriculum and services. These differences reflect, in part, the responsiveness of these colleges to the educational needs of diverse communities and student bodies. The differences also result from inequities in planning, resources, and commitments. To the extent that these deficiencies are widespread among colleges, they define gaps in the community college program and failure to achieve institutional goals.

The particular components of the comprehensive program which are generally underdeveloped are career guidance, special help to the undereducated, and community service. Compared with other functions of the program, these three lack full staff commitment, effective planning, and adequate resources.

Program balance and integration. Little attention has been given to the interrelationship and interdependency of the several components of the community college program. There are efforts to facilitate student redirection within a varied curriculum. Remedial programs, with modest success, seek to prepare students for college-level work; and certain community service activities can be considered as "outreach" to segments of the community which might subsequently be served by other parts of the college program. However, few community college educators would claim that the present allocation of resources reflects carefully weighed priorities. Guidance and developmental education, as well as certain types of occupational curricula, are undersupported, while transfer education consumes the lion's share of the instructional budget. This is so in spite of the modest rates of transfer to senior institutions, irrational counselor-student ratios, and heavy drop-out rates for precisely the students whom the community colleges claim to serve.

Program organization. A widespread consequence of the explosive growth of community colleges and the tensions resulting from the incongruence of institutional claims and practices is the reexamination of institutional structures for program leadership and development. There is general discontent with both the laissez-faire and segmented departmental structures of traditional higher education and the hierarchical and authoritarian heritage from public secondary education. New internal structures (divisions, career teams, mini-colleges, senates) are replacing governance patterns which seem dysfunctional to the highly interdependent components of the program of this new institution. External structures (super-boards, multicampus systems, interdistrict coordination) are developing at a rapid pace and have profound implications. It is possible that as organizational changes take place, concerns for comprehensiveness of program and the achievement of community college goals may be secondary to such related issues as utilization of scarce resources, distribution of power, response to student and faculty discontent, and compromises within emerging systems of post-secondary education.

There is danger that institutional and program reorganization will result less from rational planning to achieve explicitly defined goals than from accommodating conflicting power structures and efforts to disguise business as usual.

Commitment to the comprehensive program. Whether the community college can and will maintain a sufficiently comprehensive program as a means of serving its diverse student body is still an unanswered question. The community college movement is, in effect, being led by a small and highly influential group. They have—out of practice and idealism—a compelling orthodoxy regarding equality of educational opportunity beyond high school and have developed program innovations to achieve such goals. But there is by no means universal commitment to these democratic goals, either at the faculty or state planning levels. Frequently, the incongruence is between casual agreement to a general educational philosophy and resistance to putting such philosophy into practice. Such resistance is frequently the result of not knowing how to achieve such demanding educational objectives, rather than not wanting to do so. Nevertheless, there are those within and without the institution who are unsympathetic to the social and educational goals of the community college.

Faculty resistance and faltering commitment to specific components of the program and to the concept of comprehensiveness may result, in part, from inadequate involvement of faculty leadership in setting institutional goals and in program development. Without such commitment the community college will not emerge from junior status in an education game dominated by elite universities.

Inadequate State Master Planning In most of the states in which master plans for postsecondary education have been developed, the public two-year college has a prominent place. The tendency for this to occur is increasing. Also, these plans tend to place this type of institution within the context of higher education and detail the conditions for its development. Yet, as Cross (1969) has commented, "it is almost impossible to arrive at a national picture of junior college progress by reading state master plans." Hurlburt's analysis (1969) of planning for community colleges in 50 states supports the opinion that while most of the states now have specifications for the development of two-year colleges, the plans are frequently not well integrated with an overall plan for education beyond the high school. Furthermore, they too often deal with broad generalities and do not provide enough guidance to help the community college achieve its assigned mission. It seems inconceivable that, with almost one-third of all beginning college students entering community colleges, almost every state would not have taken firm steps by now toward shaping a plan for such colleges within the context of all postsecondary education.

Staffing the Community College

Evidence in Chapter 6 projects the difficult problem ahead in recruiting, training, and providing in-service assistance to community college teaching and counseling staffs. With the growth in the number of individuals completing advanced degree programs, the problem will eventually become less related to quantity than to quality as measured by the staff members' interest and belief in the mission of the community college and their ability to work effectively with its clientele. In many ways the situation is just as acute with respect to administrative staff, for unless the community college can find administrators with commitment, social sensitivity, and skill, it can hardly be expected to achieve its avowed purposes.

An important element of the problem will be to identify staff members whose interests and background will enable them to relate meaningfully to the increasing number of students who are "new" to postsecondary education. Since the majority of such students will fall below the median in academic aptitude as measured by conventional means and a high percentage of them will come from homes low on the socioeconomic scale, the staff will need a deep commitment to the belief that such students have a place in the college and that means can be found to retain them under conditions profitable to them. It is especially important that the staff have a strong orientation to the special situations involved in working with students from ethnic minority groups. Much can and must be accomplished by the recruitment and preparation of staff from these groups, but this alone is insufficient. Unless the *entire* staff has such an orientation, it is difficult to see how an urban college can serve the ethnic components of its community.

Since the emphasis of the faculty must be on teaching rather than on research, the preparation of community college teachers is not necessarily the same as that for faculty in four-year institutions. Whether a truly effective program for their preparation can be developed is still a moot, but highly significant, question. The problem of preparing a sufficient number of effective counselors and other understanding student personnel workers is just as great and is one to which inadequate attention is given.

But as important as the preparation and recruitment of a dynamic new staff may be, these efforts must be supplemented by a program which enables those now employed in the community college to understand and cope with the problems this institution faces as it moves into the decade of the 70s. Many changes in the expectations held of the community college by its clientele, particularly in urban communities, have only recently occurred, and more are in the offing. Yet many present faculty members do not subscribe to the wide range of community college goals or to its egalitarian nature. It could be, then, that the viability of the community college as an instrument for change could be endangered by this lack of congruity between institutional goals as imposed by society and the values held by the staff. No single solution is suggested since obviously the problem must be attacked by individual colleges, with assistance from professional associations and the colleges and universities involved in leadership training programs.

Strengthening State and Local Government There is no agreement on the ideal method for planning and controlling community colleges, nor is there consensus that any one plan should necessarily be adopted by all 50 states. On the other hand, the present diversity of patterns among the states raises a question of whether many of the governance arrangements may have resulted more from provincialism than from a consideration of appropriate alternatives. As reported in Chapter 6, these patterns range all the way from a high degree of local autonomy to complete state control. Further, in a number of states the major state university—or in some instances several universities—purportedly discharge the community college function by establishing lower-division centers in local communities.

The final determination of a governance pattern in a given state will obviously be based on a number of considerations. One is the degree to which local autonomy is considered desirable. Another is the extent to which it is believed that some agency should possess the authority to plan, coordinate, and even make final decisions regarding the direction of community college education for a state as a whole. A third is an opinion as to whether the community college functions can best be discharged by separately organized units or as adjuncts of a university. As implied and expressed in Chapter 7, there are seemingly valid arguments for a strong role on the part of the state, otherwise there can be no guarantee that the needs of all the people will be met. But there are also strong arguments in favor of local involvement, and regardless of the form of organization in a given state, there is need for a mechanism which provides for a joint decision-making process between those who see the community college as an integral part of their community and those who must assess it from the standpoint of the total system of postsecondary education.

Whether universities, through a system of extension centers, by whatever name such centers are labeled, can fulfill the role of the community college is also still a moot question. In several states in which all the public two-year institutions are operated by a university, there has recently been either a recommendation from a study group or other pressures to separate these institutions from the university structure. In most cases, there is resistance by the university, and thus the present system is continued. In states such as Ohio and Pennsylvania, a limited number of community colleges have been established as parallel institutions to the university centers. In the study on which this volume is based, no attempt was made to evaluate the comparative merits of the two systems.

Adequate Financial Support
As with all educational institutions, community colleges could profit from increased financial support despite the fact that currently they have fewer problems in this respect than do private junior colleges. In general, community colleges appear to have gained a reasonable level of support, although not without considerable persistence. However, variations in the level of support among states and regions, as well as in the proportions of state and local aid where the support is shared, create significant problems. In too many instances, the burden on the local community is excessive. In times of increasing resistance to realty taxes and other sources of local revenue, the willingness of the public to support increases in operating and capital funds shows signs of waning. At the same time, the pressure to reduce expenditures is evident in many states, and the community college may be entering a period of considerable financial difficulty. There are three strong arguments in favor of increased state support for community colleges: it tends to equalize the burden of community college support, it draws on funds from sources other than property taxes, and it places the funding of community colleges on somewhat the same footing as other public higher education. Undoubtedly, a greater proportion of the total revenue required for the community college will, in the future, come from state sources than has been true in the past. The future role of the federal government in this

respect is still unknown, but judging from its recent interest in the community college, it, too, will become an increasing source of revenue. In fact, it is unlikely that institutional, personnel, and program development suggested in previous chapters will take place without such federal assistance.

An unresolved problem of community college support lies with the issue of tuition. Many claims are made for its being tuition-free, yet, in most states, tuition is imposed and in some instances is derived by a formula that makes the amount so high that the concept of equal opportunity is voided. Clearly, the issue of what charges should be imposed on community college students is one which must be settled soon. At this time, when the community college is the subject of searching reexamination, the matter of student cost is paramount in assessing its potential future role. If the principle of tuition becomes established now, it is likely to persist.

RECOMMENDA-TIONS   If junior colleges are to realize their potential in the decade ahead, innumerable individuals and many agencies will have to take positive action in various directions. The precise nature of these actions naturally will vary according to the perception of the individuals who will take them, but in view of the issues outlined above the following recommendations seem imperative:

1   *The junior colleges—specifically members of governing boards, administrators, and faculty—should reassess their goals and the means of attaining them.*

In the case of the independent institutions the appraisal should enable each one to articulate and interpret to the public its uniqueness and its reason for being, for no longer can it be "just another two-year college." It is hoped that the financial dilemma of those institutions can be alleviated in part by some of the suggestions offered subsequently, but even for this to happen, the appeal to the public must be in terms of how the college can serve students in a way that other institutions do not. And it will have to be mindful of changing societal values and the fact that the majority of high school graduates today are in quest of personal freedom, opportunity for self-expression and -reliance, and the liberty to question existing mores. The "finishing school" concept is no longer viable, and while certain occupational training at a reasonably high level of sophistication is expected in some of the independent colleges, even that must be supplemented by educational and personal experiences that will ordinarily not be obtainable in other institutions.

The public community colleges bear an exceedingly heavy responsibility to assess themselves. Even if all the conditions for the sound development and support of community colleges were optimum, the expectations which the nation has placed on this institution as a means of equalizing educational opportunity could be lost for want of programs for students whose abilities, backgrounds, and interests are as diverse as those of a high school senior class. The ostrich stance regarding such matters as high student attrition rates is not tolerable in these times. There is overriding concern about the preparation of students to transfer, when not more than half of those who declare such intentions ever do so, and about negative attitudes on the part of many staff members toward programs and services for the nontransfer students. The community colleges cannot be equated with "college" in the traditional sense. Thus it is imperative that each community college develop an enthusiasm for a new mission. If the colleges fail to do this, it is probable that other types of nonbaccalaureate institutions will be established to perform some of the services which they are presumed to render, but on which they will have defaulted.

Greater faculty commitment to community college program development will require (1) opportunities for faculty to study new approaches to curriculum and instruction and to try new models; (2) systematic faculty involvement in the decision-making process at the campus and interinstitutional levels; and (3) the development of new programs in American universities to prepare community college faculty for understanding the institution and for contributing to its development.

Among the leaders in American education are some who believe that the community college cannot deliver on its comprehensive function. Furthermore, already there are numerous types of postsecondary, prebaccalaureate institutions in operation, and in the American pluralistic system it is probable that additional types, both public and private, will question both the extent of the duplication and the reliance it has placed on the community college as a comprehensive institution.

2 *Each state should review its basic plan for community colleges within the context of all postsecondary education.*

It is unwise for a state to develop a long-term plan for community colleges — no matter how good the plan — and not make it an integral part of a system for *all* education beyond high school. The special missions of each institutional type and the interrelationships among them must be explicit. Perhaps the most important consideration in formulating a state master plan is that of eliminating barriers to post-high school education. This necessitates a review of factors such as:

a Proximity of educational programs to students' homes

b Cost of education to the student

c Availability of programs which attract students, particularly those in highly urbanized areas who are not now being served

d Realism in institutional goals and resources, i.e., whether given institutions are prepared to fulfill the mission expected of them

The mission of the four-year colleges and the universities — whether self-adopted or assigned — is not likely to serve the needs of the total society. Thus, if barriers are to be greatly reduced, strong arguments exist for the community college which takes education to the people and is either tuition-free or of minimal cost to students. But since access to post-high school education is also dependent upon whether a student can find a program to suit him, a determination must be made of which institutions are to offer which programs. Given the general premise that four-year institutions must be concerned primarily with conventional degree work, many other activities must fall to the community colleges. In recent years senior institutions have had a tendency under pressure to initiate new programs for the disadvantaged, and even to lower admission standards for the undereducated. However, good questions arise as to whether in the long run these modifications will be continued. As already indicated, the community college has also been questioned regarding its ability to serve unconventional needs, but if this task is specifically assigned to it under a state plan, the chances of its being filled are better than if left to those institutions whose historical assignment has been more conventional.

State plans for community colleges tend to deal primarily with structure and support, but not enough of them are explicit about the purpose and nature of the community colleges and their relationships to other institutions.

Individual institutions and the several states should develop educational master plans which stress the maximum development of students within coordinated systems. New concepts of coordination with the secondary schools and advanced institutions should have these goals as central concerns, rather than traditional chauvinistic concerns for course parallelism and program similarity. Research and development programs will be needed to focus on problems which cut across systems of institutions. It is likely that legislation will be needed to provide the impetus and resources for such development and for implementing the innovations which may be recommended.

State plans for community colleges need to be specific with reference to several issues. They must, for example, provide the general guidelines for the establishment of new institutions so that most high school graduates will live within commuting distance of a community college. They must provide both the impetus and the framework for the development of career programs in community colleges. This is a complex task where state agency response for vocational-technical programs is separate from the governance structure for community colleges. But in such situations there must either be some type of amalgamation of agencies or some superstructure that provides for the necessary statewide development and coordination of occupational education.

The proper functioning of a guidance program in community colleges is still another area of concern for state planning. It may be that such a program cannot be mandated, but its designation as a prime community college function and incentives for its financial support can and should be detailed as a means of aiding individual colleges in initiating and maintaining a strong program.

Because questions concerning the optimum size of community colleges arise continuously, state plans should from their inception provide general guidelines with respect to minimum and optimum enrollment. The authors agree with the Carnegie Commission's position that the range of optimum size is between 2,000 and 5,000 daytime students, but they also recognize that new organizational patterns within institutions make it feasible for many individual institutions, particularly those in urban centers, to become considerably larger.

Finally, a state plan must provide definite assurance that students desiring to transfer from a community college will have top priority for admission to public four-year institutions in the state. Without such a provision, the entire community college structure is on shaky ground, since students who are encouraged to attend a two-year college may be penalized later by admission practices in four-year institutions which preclude their transfer. Thus, the plan for articulation must be clear and binding.

Inter- and intrainstitutional studies are called for to determine the evolving needs of students and communities in all aspects of the community college program. It is particularly important that model programs be developed which envision systematic evaluation and dissemination to other colleges. Such research, and the use of new management technologies, should contribute to the operational definition and effective evaluation of program objectives.

3 *Each state should review its structure for governing its community colleges.*

Given the desirability of a pluralistic approach so that a given state may decide whether its community colleges are under the complete jurisdiction of the state or are subject to local control with a degree of state supervision, it is highly important that there be a viable organization for their coordination and direction. Appropriate machinery must be set up as a means of ensuring their efficiency, their relevance, and their appropriate role in the entire state program of education. Most states appear to be moving in the direction of greater centralization of control of community colleges, and this may indeed be the only feasible means of providing the necessary guarantee that the community college will become functional.

4 *New means should be found for financial support of community colleges.*

The financial responsibility of the local community should be reduced by increasing the support by the states and the federal government. This shift in support becomes mandatory in view of current strains on local tax funds and the variation in the ability of local communities to support postsecondary education. The nation as a whole has a distinct stake in an institution that equalizes educational opportunity. Legislation pending in Congress, as well as various task forces currently at work in the executive branch, indicates the interest of the federal government in the community college. But interest must eventually be coupled with support. State governments also have a vested interest and no longer should expect local taxing bodies to assume a cost (which in some instances runs as high as two-thirds of the total) for educating students in the community college, while states pay the total cost (exclusive of tuition and fees) of the four-year colleges and universities.

5   *Additional support must be obtained for aid to community college students.*

In a sense this is a new concept in higher education, but it is particularly relevant since the majority of community college students need funds to enable them to remain in school. Yet, ironically, financial aid to them is more limited than for students in other institutions. Again, much of the help must come from state and federal sources through scholarship funds or other direct grants as already proposed by the Carnegie Commission on Higher Education and other agencies. However, each community college can help by a continuous campaign for private funds to use at its discretion in aiding students. It is unlikely that loan funds will be as appealing to community college students as to those in four-year colleges because of differences in the socioeconomic backgrounds of the two groups.

New concepts of, as well as resources for, student financial aid are needed. Much research is now available to guide state and federal planners as to the diversity of student needs and attitudes. Of particular importance in programs to serve junior college students is the potency of social class attitudes toward borrowing to finance education. There is ample evidence that poor families generally, and minority families specifically, are reluctant to accrue such indebtedness. Of equal importance is the need to consider foregone earnings and the amount of work for pay which can be tolerated for students who are marginal as a result of financial, academic, and personal pressures.

6   *Financing of independent junior colleges must be placed on a sounder basis than at present.*

In states where public funds are available to private institutions generally, the two-year institutions should share the assistance according to criteria and plans established by the state. Another form of assistance is possible by a federal program of aid to students, coupled with grants to institutions for the cost of educating additional students. Without additional assistance the days of many independent junior colleges are numbered, and while there should be no crusade merely to keep *all* private two-year colleges alive, the best ones should be preserved for the significant contribution they can make.

7   *There should be a nationwide drive to prepare and develop faculty and administrators for the junior colleges.*

The need in terms of quantity, though great, is not as acute as for staff with the competencies to teach and administer in a unique institution. Various professional associations, state and federal agencies, and colleges and universities all have a stake in this important task. Certain foundations have been generous in their support of special programs in helping professional groups to determine new approaches and goals. This has helped, but the effort has only begun.

Regardless of the exact form which this program takes and irrespective of whether the target is teaching staff, student personnel workers, or administrators, three elements should be integral to the total effort. First, there should be a careful delineation of staff needs in terms of job requirements and of the personal and educational characteristics of the staff necessary to fulfill the requirements. Second, strong consideration should be given to the recruitment of potential staff from among the representative segments of the population, particularly, ethnic minority groups. Third, the preparation program should, to the extent possible, include significant supervised observational and work experiences in the junior college. For teaching and student personnel staff, the widely discussed Doctorate of Arts degree may have considerable validity, although its feasibility still has to be determined.

Recent efforts on the part of the American Association of Junior Colleges to serve as a catalytic agency in identifying and monitoring programs of staff development are to be commended, but they must be continued in a way that involves the U.S. Office of Education, the several foundations, the various state agencies, the many colleges and universities engaged in staff preparation, and the junior colleges themselves.

The two-year college movement has made significant strides during the first six decades of the twentieth century. Without doubt, however, its supreme test is yet to come, perhaps during the seventies. Almost certainly the period immediately ahead will bring profound social changes, and there will be a need (that exceeds even that of prior years) for an institution like the community college. For it to respond to these changes will require the greatest possible input on the part of those within the institution as well as of persons who occupy leadership positions in government and other segments of education. Planning must be done and appropriate staff prepared. Adequate resources must become available and the public's understanding of the two-year college role must increase. The process will require time, understanding, and cooperation on the part of students, faculty, administrators, board members, legislators, and the public at large. The potential of the two-year college to revitalize American education is high, and it is waiting to be realized fully.

Commentary

The authors of *Breaking the Access Barriers* have introduced to the reader the heterogeneity of the two-year colleges as well as the heterogeneity of the students enrolled. The three cameo sketches in Chapter 1 are clearly indicative of the great diversity among community colleges, associated with the many variables which are discussed in detail. This emphasis on diversity is of prime importance, for too many forces, both within and without educational circles, would bring pressures to bear on the need to homogenize the community colleges into institutions resembling their four-year brothers. This is especially true of those who believe in the status of the meritocratic college versus the egalitarian philosophy of the democratized community college.

The authors have devoted most of their material to an in-depth study of the community college and its relationship to students, to the community, and to the other segments of higher education, or, as they say preferably, to postsecondary education. The research is specific and plentiful and brings to the reader a wealth of information from which he can draw his own conclusions. Certainly, the authors have provided a great service to both educators and lay citizens by bringing together in one publication facts, figures, and pro and con discussions concerning the role of the community college—yesterday, today, and as projected for tomorrow.

The reader must be patient, however, as he waits for the authors' conclusions and recommendations. These are stated with strength and conciseness in the final pages of the publication; special attention should be given to the seven specific recommendations, all of which are of the utmost importance if the two-year postsecondary community or junior college is to fulfill its stated objectives.

The first recommendation deals with the need for governing

155

boards, administrators, and faculty to reassess their goals and the means of attaining them. This recommendation is paramount, and the authors are to be commended for placing it in the top-priority position. Most of the two-year colleges have clearly stated goals in their various publications, but in far too many cases these goals are limited to printed words only. Harold Hodgkinson in his recent report *Institutions In Transition*[1] points out the trend for collegiate institutions increasingly to resemble one another— whether they are public or independent, two-year or four-year. If this is true, and I believe it is, the great need for diversity among colleges, the need for a pluralistic approach, will be lost, and colleges will be serving a rather well-defined, select group, even though their stated goals read otherwise.

The boards, administrators, and faculty of the community colleges have been charged by their communities and states to provide educational opportunities for those youth and adults who have need for and can profit from postsecondary education. From this charge, the community colleges have called themselves "peoples' colleges"—colleges for all the people, where students can benefit culturally, socially, and occupationally. These colleges, on paper, advocate that the institution is a cultural center, a lower-division academic center, a career training center, a counseling center, a center for overcoming scholastic deficiencies, a continuing education and community service center—for all within commuting distance. Many of the colleges in addition provide dormitories for those students who live too far away to commute.

These are great objectives, for, if met, the colleges will become change agents for the life of the community, the state, and the nation as a whole.

We agree today that the availability for all of elementary education and, later, of secondary education was the prime factor for the almost unbelievable development of this country. Other countries, seeing the results of mass education, have emulated us educationally and are following us developmentally. Countries where such education is a privilege for the few are treading the degrading waters of illiteracy, and they remain poverty-stricken and underdeveloped except for a small percentage of the elite.

We now agree, on paper, that postsecondary education is also a right and not a privilege for those who are so motivated and can

---

[1] Prepared for the Carnegie Commission on Higher Education, Berkeley, 1970.

profit from the opportunity to grow culturally, socially, and occupationally. We agree that this growth of the individual permits self-fulfillment and, therefore, benefits all of society through the positive contributions of the individual. Such contributions create cultural, social, and economic wealth. The loss of such contributions, through the failure to provide the opportunities for individual growth, creates a diametrically opposed force—a force which consumes cultural, social, and economic wealth. The logic of this argument, as alluded to throughout this profile, is amazingly simple —and yet there are so many of us, educators and lay citizens alike, who would prefer to leave the logic and goals on paper and continue to act in a meritocratic manner where status, the false status of academic superiority, is the acceptable action.

The leadership, the faculty, the boards must be committed to the democratization of the community colleges' instructional program if these are to be "open-door" colleges in truth instead of fiction. Apology programs in career education, developmental learning, continuing education, community service, and counseling and guidance will not suffice. The emphasis primarily on academic transfer programs, with anemic attention paid to the other stated goals, must of necessity transform the open-door concept into a "revolving-door" actuality. This type of intellectual dishonesty is chicanery, to say the least, and leads only to cynicism on the part of the students and citizens who had hoped for personal growth through the accessibility of the community college.

The authors' inference that some other institution will undertake to assume some of these goals if the community colleges fail to meet the challenge is well founded. Already we see evidence of business and industry entering the field of education, and of a transfer of confidence among citizens from educators to business and industry on the basis of pragmatism.

Those who criticize the comprehensiveness of the community college have stated and continue to state that the community college tries to be all things to all people. Such critics are usually ignorant about the college, quite often have never been on the campus of a first-rate comprehensive institution, and are probably mired down in the meritocratic tradition. The tragedy is that they are listened to by too many of their peers and (even more tragically) by too many board members, administrators, and faculty of the community colleges themselves.

The authors state well their concerns about the viability of the comprehensive community college during the decade ahead. These concerns must be faced honestly. The boards, administrators, and faculty must without question have the integrity to support actually, and not just verbally, the philosophy as stated. All involved must see clearly the real status of the community college—a status different from that of a university, but a status of greater importance to the people who make up the community served by the college.

Much of the status of a university is built around its graduate schools and the research associated with such schools. This status is justified, for the contributions to society are great. The numbers of students served, however, are small in comparison with the cost to the average citizen through taxation and tuition costs for undergraduate students. The university has its goals, and these are accepted with accompanying status.

The community college in its comprehensiveness has its own status of service to people; here, equal access to a quality postsecondary education is a contribution second to none in the field of higher education. In addition to this, however, there must also be a research factor as in the university. The research in the community college must be in the area of teaching. The open-door, equal-access philosophy brings into the college students who need individualized instruction, and this mandates a change from the generally practiced chalk-talk, lecture, note-taking methods followed by so many generations of teachers.

As the authors state, teachers and administrators for tomorrow's community colleges must know how to teach and how to provide the leadership so urgently needed. Few of these individuals have had the opportunity in graduate schools to have the actual experience required to cope successfully with the demands of the college. A community college teacher cannot emulate his graduate school professor and hope to "reach" his students. The teacher and administrators must together work toward student achievement through teaching methods, grading practices, individualized instruction, advanced placement tests, and adequate counseling and guidance. It is hoped that increased attention will be given by graduate schools in the area of internships—both for faculty and administrators. Internship programs, where the teacher or administrator is fully immersed, totally involved for at least one semester in a truly comprehensive community college, will permit the colleges to recruit staff members who are already committed to the profession they have chosen. They will have their status and will be proud of their choice.

The authors' discussion of statewide master planning, state control, and local control is most pertinent to the expansion of community colleges and to the role they must play in higher education. As stated, no one plan is a panacea, but evidence needs to be accumulated and disseminated with respect to successes and failures. The Carnegie Commission report *The Open-Door Colleges* (June, 1970) recommends strongly in favor of the need for state master planning and local control and against the establishment of more two-year branches of universities or more two-year technical institutes. Agreement must be reached in the various states if the proliferation of weak or narrowly defined institutions is to be avoided. Too many states waited too long for analysis and planning and are now faced with cleaning up the chaos which resulted from their neglect. Strong colleges which serve local needs and which provide statewide access are required to fulfill the objective of equal opportunity, and these should be supported financially in order to achieve the comprehensiveness which reflects the open-door philosophy. However, the proliferation of weak or narrowly defined two-year institutions is costly to both student and taxpayer. The students do not receive the educational opportunities which are available in a strong, comprehensive institution; the taxpayers are paying high costs for the politics of campus proliferation and for the resultant unnecessary duplication of effort.

The politicization of colleges by the students and/or faculty is unacceptable. Also unacceptable is the politicization of community colleges by location or through board of trustees appointment and action. The responsibility of the state and local leadership for today's 2 million community college students and tomorrow's 3 million students is too great not to have settled on master plans for the location and financing of the present 1,050 two-year colleges and the proposed 230 to 280 additional two-year colleges by 1980. There must be a plan defining the function, structure, and financing of postsecondary education for each of the 50 states of which the community college as a comprehensive institution is an integral part. Any continued lack of planning can only be defined as irresponsibility on the part of the state leadership, both executive and legislative, and on the part of the educational leaders who knowingly or unknowingly continue to use unilateral action as the modus operandi.

The suspicion of higher education prevalent among too many citizens today, will not permit the luxury of political and unilateral actions. The mandate is for planning and cooperative effort if higher education from community colleges through the graduate schools is to provide the services asked for by today's student and today's taxpayer.

The authors reemphasize with good effect the points of emphasis in the first three reports of the Carnegie Commission[2] with respect to both college financing and student financing. It is important to note the authors' emphasis on the need for student financial help where foregone earnings would prevent students from low-income families from attending college. The open-door, equal-access philosophy may well be a fiction for the low-income students and just another advantage for the middle- and higher-income students —even though the low-income taxpayer helps pay the taxes which support the community colleges.

Grants or loans must be available if equal access is to become a reality for those who wish to enroll and can profit from the educational offerings.

The independent junior college has played and continues to play an important role in postsecondary education. Although, as the authors point out, most of the enrollment growth during the past 25 years has been in the public institutions, the independent junior colleges have maintained and even expanded their total enrollments. Many of these colleges are strong and will continue to be so, thus serving their constituencies well. At the same time some weaker institutions may well be unable to cope with the financial recruitment and staffing problems and will have to terminate their operations. As is the case with all collegiate institutions, both two- and four-year weak institutions may well be doing a disservice to their students if they are unable to provide strong educational programs. This applies to public community colleges as well as to independent junior colleges.

Since most independent junior colleges are not comprehensive in nature, their enrollments can be lower, but even so there has to be some recognized minimum enrollment if the college is to

[2] *Quality and Equality: Revised Recommendations—New Levels of Federal Responsibility for Higher Education* (a supplement to the 1968 Special Report), 1970; *A Chance to Learn: An Action Agenda for Equal Opportunity in Higher Education,* 1970; *The Open-Door Colleges: Policies for Community Colleges,* McGraw-Hill Book Company, New York, 1970.

attract students, staff, and the necessary finances in order to survive.

The authors' concurrence with the Carnegie Commission's findings in *The Open-Door Colleges,* namely, that the optimum enrollment in a public, comprehensive community college is from 2,000 to 5,000 full-time day students, is of importance to master planners. Enrolling fewer students too often prevents the financing of sequential classes, career curricula, developmental instruction, strong counseling programs, and research and development. Enrolling more students tends to impersonalize the college, and fragmentation within the faculty often follows—with subsequent fragmentation of the student body. These results need not occur if there are sufficient financial resources for the smaller college and sufficient student-centered leadership for the larger institutions.

CONCLUSION   Leland Medsker and Dale Tillery have contributed a research document which will be utilized as resource material by boards, administrators, faculty, and graduate students for years to come. Leaders in government—local, state, and national—will also benefit and will take actions based upon their data, discussion, and recommendations. We have been greatly in need of this summary; and yet an updating will also be needed, by not later than 1975. As stated so well in the conclusion, "The supreme test is yet to come, perhaps during the seventies."

Joseph P. Cosand

References

American Association of Junior Colleges: *1969 Junior College Directory,* Washington, D.C., 1969.

Anderson, E. F., and C. E. Thornblod: *Report of Selected Data and Characteristics, Illinois Public Junior Colleges, 1968–69,* Illinois Report No. 19, Illinois Junior College Board, Springfield, 1969.

Arney, L. H.: "A Comparison of Patterns of Financial Support with Selected Criteria in Community Junior Colleges," unpublished doctoral dissertation, University of Florida, 1969.

Astin, A. W., R. J. Panos, and J. A. Creager: *National Norms for Entering College Freshmen—Fall, 1966,* American Council on Education Research Reports, vol. 2, no. 1, 1967.

Beazley, R.: "Number and Characteristics of Employees in Institutions of Higher Education, Fall, 1966," *Digest of Educational Statistics,* U.S. Office of Education, 1969.

Berg, Ernest H., and Dayton Axtell: *Programs for Disadvantaged Students in the California Community Colleges,* Peralta Junior College District, Oakland, 1968.

Berg, E.: "Selected Factors Bearing on the Persistence and Academic Performance of Low-Ability Students in Four California Junior Colleges," unpublished doctoral dissertation, University of California, Berkeley, 1965.

Bowles, F., and F. DeCosta: *Between Two Worlds: A Profile of Negro Higher Education,* McGraw-Hill Book Company, New York, to be published for the Carnegie Commission on Higher Education, 1971.

California Coordinating Council for Education: *Financial Assistance to California College and University Students,* Staff Report 67-13, Sacramento, August, 1967.

California Junior College Association: *Implementing the Open Door,* Report No. 2, Foothill College, Los Altos, 1964.

Carnegie Commission on Higher Education: *The Open-Door Colleges: Policies for Community Colleges,* special report, McGraw-Hill Book Company, New York, June, 1970.

Chalghian, S.: "Success for Marginal Students," *Junior College Journal,* vol. 40, no. 1, pp. 28–30, 1969.

Clark, B. R.: *The Open Door College,* McGraw-Hill Book Company, New York, 1960.

Collins, C. C.: *Junior College Student Personnel Programs—What They Are and What They Should Be,* American Association of Junior Colleges, Washington, D.C., 1967.

Collins, C. C.: "Some Student Characteristics and Their Implications for Student Personnel Work," in Terry O'Banion and Alice Thirsten, *Junior College Student Personnel Work: Practice and Potential,* Prentice-Hall, Inc., Englewood Cliffs, N.J., 1970.

Collins, C. C., and J. J. Collins: *The Case for the Community College: A Critical Appraisal of Philosophy and Function,* published by the authors, El Cajon, Calif., 1966.

Cooley, W. W., and S. J. Becker: "The Junior College Student," *Personnel and Guidance Journal,* vol. 44, no. 5, pp. 464–469, January, 1966.

Cooper, R. M.: "The College Teaching Crisis," *Journal of Higher Education,* vol. 35, pp. 6–11, 1964.

Cosand, J. P.: Paper (untitled) presented to California Junior College Association Convention, Los Angeles, Oct. 22, 1969.

Cross, K. P.: *The Junior College Students: A Research Description,* Educational Testing Service, Princeton, N.J., 1968.

Cross, K. P.: *The Junior College's Role in Providing Postsecondary Education for All,* prepared for the U.S. Office of Education, Washington, D.C., 1969.

Cross, K. P.: Unpublished study of Community Colleges' Programs for Poorly Prepared Students, Center for Research and Development in Higher Education, Berkeley, 1970.

Darley, J. G.: *Promise and Performance: A Study of Ability and Achievement in Higher Education,* Center for the Study of Higher Education, University of California, Berkeley, 1962.

DeHart, Robert A.: *An Open Door to What? Implementing the Open Door,* California Junior College Association Committee on Personnel and Guidance Report No. 2, Asilomar, 1964.

Diablo Valley Junior College: *Catalogue 1969–1970,* Pleasant Hill, Calif., 1969–1970.

Feldman, M.: Unpublished position paper for U.S. Commissioner of Education, U.S. Office of Education, Washington, D.C., 1969.

Froomkin, J.: *Aspirations, Enrollments, and Resources,* planning paper 69-1, Office of Planning and Evaluation, U.S. Office of Education, Washington, D.C., May, 1969.

Fryer, T.: *Draft Statement of Campus Objectives,* Miami Dade Junior College, Miami, 1969.

Garrison, R. H.: *Junior College Faculty: Issues and Problems—A Preliminary National Appraisal,* American Association of Junior Colleges, Washington, D.C., 1967.

Garrison, R. H.: "Private Junior Colleges: The Question is Survival," *Junior College Journal,* vol. 39, no. 6, pp. 35–38, 1969.

Gleazer, E. J., Jr.: *This Is the Community College,* Houghton Mifflin Company, Boston, 1968.

Harlacher, E. L.: *The Community Dimension of the Community College,* Prentice-Hall, Inc., Englewood Cliffs, N.J., 1969.

Harris, N. C.: *Technical Education in the Junior College: New Programs for New Jobs,* American Association of Junior Colleges, Washington, D.C., 1964.

Hendrix, V. L.: "Academic Rank? Mostly Peril?" *Junior College Journal,* vol. 35, no. 4, pp. 28–30, 1963–1964.

Hendrix, V. L.: "Academic Rank Revisited," *Junior College Journal,* vol. 35, no. 5, pp. 24–28, 1965.

Hooker, Thomas: *Report on the Faculties Development Project,* American Association of Junior Colleges, Washington, D.C., 1969.

Hurlburt, A. S.: *State Master Plans for Community Colleges,* American Association of Junior Colleges, Washington, D.C., 1969.

Johnson, B. L.: *General Education in Action,* American Council on Education, Washington, D.C., 1952.

Johnson, B. L.: *Islands of Innovation Expanding: Changes in the Community College,* Glencoe Press, Beverly Hills, 1969.

Kerr, C.: "The Urban Grant University," *The City College Papers, 8,* New York, 1968.

Knoell, D.: *Who Goes to College from the Community of the Urban Center,* Address to the 1969 Convention of the California Junior College Association, Los Angeles, Oct. 21, 1969.

Knoell, D., and L. Medsker: *Factors Affecting Performance of Transfer Students from Two- and Four-Year Colleges: With Implications for*

Coordination and Articulation, Cooperation Research Project No. 1133, Center for the Study of Higher Education, University of California, Berkeley, 1964.

Koos, L. V.: *The Junior College Movement,* Ginn and Company, Boston, 1925.

Mayhew, L. B., and P. L. Dressel: *General Education: Explorations in Evaluation,* Final Report of the Cooperative Study of Evaluation, American Council on Education, Washington, D.C., 1954.

McConnell, T. R., in C. C. Collins: *Junior College Student Personnel Programs—What They Are and What They Should Be,* American Association of Junior Colleges, Washington, D.C., 1967.

Medsker, L.: *The Junior College: Progress and Prospect,* McGraw-Hill Book Company, New York, 1960.

Medsker, L. L., and J. W. Trent: *The Influence of Different Types of Public Higher Institutions on College Attendance from Varying Socioeconomic Ability Levels,* Center for Research and Development in Higher Education, Berkeley, 1965.

Morrison, D. G., and S. V. Martorana: "State Formulas for the Support of Public Two-Year Colleges," *Office of Education Bulletin, 1962,* no. 14. U.S. Office of Education, Washington, D.C., 1962.

National Education Association: *Salaries in Higher Education, 1967–68,* Higher Education Series Research Report 1968-R7.

Peterson, J.: "Community Centeredness and Institutional Adaptability under State and Local Control: Case Studies of Two Community Colleges," unpublished doctoral dissertation, University of California, Berkeley, 1969.

Phair, T. S.: "California Colleges Look at Their New Faculty," *Junior College Journal,* vol. 39, no. 4, pp. 48–50, 1968–1969.

Raines, M.: *Junior College Student Personnel Programs: Appraisal and Development,* AAJC, supported by Carnegie study in New York, 1966.

Reynolds, J. W.: *The Comprehensive Junior College Curriculum,* McCutchan Publishing Corporation, Berkeley, 1969.

Sanford, N.: *The American College,* John Wiley & Sons, Inc., New York, 1962.

Schrag, P.: "End of the Bull Market," *Change in Higher Education,* vol. 1, no. 6, pp. 5–7, 1969.

Schultz, R. E.: *Administrators for America's Junior Colleges, Predictions of Need 1965–1980,* American Association of Junior Colleges, Washington, D.C., 1965.

Schultz, R. E.: *The Junior College President: Who and Where From?*, Address at the National Conference on the Junior College President, University of California, Los Angeles, July, 1968.

Theodorus, J.: *Crisis in Planning,* Council for Educational Faculty Planners, Columbus, Ohio, 1968.

Tillery, D.: "Academic Rank—Promise or Peril," *Junior College Journal,* vol. 33, no. 6, pp. 6–9, 1963.

Tillery, D.: "Differential Characteristics of Entering Freshmen at the University of California and Their Peers at California Junior Colleges," unpublished doctoral dissertation, University of California, Berkeley, 1964.

Tillery, D.: *School to College: Distribution and Differentiation of Youth,* Center for Research and Development in Higher Education, Berkeley, and College Entrance Examination Board, New York, Winter 1970–71.

Tillery, D., C. Collins, L. Crouchett, R. Ontiveros, and R. Tealer: *Oakland Inner-City Project of the Peralta Colleges: An Interim Appraisal,* for the U.S. Office of Education, 1969.

Tillery, D., D. Donovan, and B. Sherman: *SCOPE Four-State Profiles, Grade Twelve, 1966, California, Illinois, Massachusetts, North Carolina,* The Center for Research and Development in Higher Education and College Entrance Examination Board, New York, 1966.

Tillery, D., D. Donovan, and B. Sherman: *SCOPE Grade Eleven Profile 1968 Questionnaire Selected Items,* Center for Research and Development in Higher Education and College Entrance Examination Board, New York, 1968.

Turnbull, W. W.: *Relevance in Testing,* paper prepared for presentation at the meeting of Commission on Tests of the College Entrance Examination Board, New York, Oct. 17–18, 1967.

U.S. Office of Education: *Opening Fall Enrollments in Higher Education, Part A—Summary,* Washington, D.C., 1968.

Van Der Ryn, S.: "The University Environment—Present and Future," unpublished paper, School of Architecture, University of California, 1969.

Venn, G.: *Man, Education, and Work,* American Council on Education, Washington, D.C., 1964.

Williams, H. A.: "Introduction of Comprehensive Community College Act of 1969," *Congressional Record,* vol. 115, no. 26, Feb. 17, 1969.

Willingham, Warren W.: "The Importance of Relevance in Expanding Postsecondary Education," *Trends in Postsecondary Education,* U.S. Office of Education, Washington, D.C., 1969.

Wilson, L.: "Merit and Equality in Higher Education," *Educational Record,* vol. 51, no. 1, pp. 5–13, 1970.

Yarrington, R.: *Junior Colleges: 50 States/50 Years,* American Association of Junior Colleges, Washington, D.C., 1969.

Appendix: Number of Two-Year Institutions of Higher Education by Type and State, 1968

State	Total	Community colleges		Two-year branches of universities*	Specialized two-year institutes	
		Public	Private		Public	Private
United States	1072	584	258	127	73	30
Alabama	19	15	4			
Alaska	7		1	6		
Arizona	9	8	1			
Arkansas	5	3	1	1		
California	90	86	2			2
Colorado	10	10				
Connecticut	25	9	7	5	4	
Delaware	4	1	3			
District of Columbia	5	1	3			1
Florida	33	27	6			
Georgia	21	12	7	1	1	
Hawaii	8		1	6		1
Idaho	5	2	3			
Illinois	58	42	14			2
Indiana	9	1	2	6†		
Iowa	25	19	4		2	
Kansas	21	17	4			
Kentucky	23		8	15		
Louisiana	6	1		3	2	
Maine	4			1		3
Maryland	20	14	6			
Massachusetts	40	14	23		1	2

State	Total	Community colleges Public	Community colleges Private	Two-year branches of universities*	Specialized two-year institutes Public	Specialized two-year institutes Private
Michigan	42	31	9			2
Minnesota	24	17	5	1		1
Mississippi	28	19	8		1	
Missouri	20	10	8			2
Montana	3	3				
Nebraska	9	6	2		1	
Nevada						
New Hampshire	4		1		3	
New Jersey	22	12	10			
New Mexico	6	3		3		
New York	67	40	24			3
North Carolina	60	13	15	3	28	1
North Dakota	6	4	1	1		
Ohio	35	5	4	21	2	3
Oklahoma	18	10	4		3	1
Oregon	16	11	4		1	
Pennsylvania	58	17	15	23	3	
Rhode Island	3	1	1			1
South Carolina	27		6	10	11	
South Dakota	2		2			
Tennessee	12	3	7		2	
Texas	51	39	11		1	
Utah	6	1		2		3
Vermont	4		2		1	1
Virginia	30	14	10	3	2	1
Washington	22	22				
West Virginia	9	1	4	4		
Wisconsin	35	15	4	12	4	
Wyoming	6	5	1			

*All two-year branches of universities are public, except for a branch of Emory University, Georgia.

†Four branch campuses of Purdue University are two-year institutions, except for a curriculum for juniors and seniors leading to a baccalaureate degree in the School of Technology.

SOURCE: U.S. Office of Education, *Education Directory 1968–69,* Part III, Washington, D.C., 1968.

Acknowledgments

The preparation of the manuscript for this publication was both exciting and difficult. It was exciting to tell the story of the two-year colleges in concise and, we hope, constructive fashion. In doing this, we felt no need to praise these emerging institutions without at the same time pointing to some of their shortcomings and suggesting ways by which they may more nearly achieve the claims made for them. The task was difficult because in the interest of brevity it was necessary to make hard decisions about what should or should not be included. The volume could have been expanded greatly, but we felt that what is needed now is a precise description and evaluation of the institutions that have so captured the imagination of the American people. This we attempted to do.

We wish to emphasize that the manuscript was the product of many sources and people. We drew heavily on recent literature and from the contributions of individuals knowledgeable about the two-year college. We also utilized data and gleaned valuable insight from two major studies of the Center for Research and Development in Higher Education at Berkeley. One of these was a recent restudy of community colleges supported by the Carnegie Corporation. The other was SCOPE—School to College: Opportunities for Postsecondary Education—funded by the College Entrance Examination Board. We are deeply indebted to the two funding agencies and to the schools and colleges participating in these studies. The staff of the Carnegie Commission on Higher Education was exceedingly helpful in many ways, and we are grateful for its assistance.

We wish also to acknowledge our debt to many of our colleagues at the Center for their assistance in various aspects of the manuscript. We are especially grateful to Norman Rae, Arthur Oswald, Gene Pratt, Denis Donovan, and Claire Almeda for the role each played in bringing the manuscript to completion.

Leland L. Medsker
Dale Tillery

Index

Outreach by junior colleges to community,
80–82

Pacesetter states:
in development of community colleges,
25–27
table of, 26
enrollment by program type, 1968 (table),
62
Part-time enrollment, 18–20
Pennsylvania:
capital outlay in (table), 121
community colleges in, development of,
22
enrollment, actual, 1968 (table), 31
funds, sources of (table), 117
junior colleges in: number of (table), 170
undergraduates in, percentage of, 1968
(table), 24
"People's college," 15, 79–80, 156
Personnel, 87–104
academic rank of, 96–97
administrators, 102–103, 111, 152
for community colleges, 143–144
degrees of, 88–89
faculties: attitudes toward institutions,
90–92
characteristics of, 87–90
numbers of, estimated, 1975 and 1980
(table), 102
and occupational education, 60–61
preparation of, 97–100, 152
work loads of, 92–94
fringe benefits for, 95–96
full-time-equivalent faculty needs (table),
101
in independent colleges, 131–132
in-service training of, 99–100
preservice training of, 97–99
projection of future needs for, 100–102
recruitment of, 89, 90, 98, 152
salaries of, 94–96
teachers, attitudes of, on occupational
education, 60–61
Politicization of colleges, 159
Population growth, effect of, on community
colleges, 13–16

Private colleges:
and community colleges, differences
between, 3
diversity of, 9–10
and public junior colleges, 47–49,
126–127
regional concentration of, 25
(*See also* Independent colleges)
Probation in developmental education, 67
Project Talent, 42
Projections of junior college growth, 27–32
Public and private junior college students,
comparison of, 47–49, 126–127
Public junior colleges (*see* Community
colleges)
Public Law 16 (*see* GI Bill of Rights)

Race (*see* Minority students)
Reading, developmental, 65
Recruitment:
of community college faculties, 89, 90, 98
of personnel, 152
of students for independent colleges, 132
Regional concentration of private junior
colleges, 25
Regional distribution of community colleges,
22, 25
Relevance of education programs, 69–70, 83
Religious colleges (*see* Church-related
colleges)
Remedial education (*see* Developmental
education)
Requirements for new colleges, 31–34
Revenues (*see* Funds)
Rhode Island:
capital outlay in (table), 121
community colleges in, controls of, 106, 108
enrollment, actual, 1968 (table), 31
funds, sources of (table), 117
junior colleges in: number of (table), 170
undergraduates in, percentage of, 1968
(table), 24
Richmond, California, 77

St. Louis, Missouri, 75–77
Salaries in community colleges, 94–96

*This book was set in Vladimir by University Graphics,
Inc. It was printed on Vellum Offset and bound by The
Maple Press Company. The designer was Elliot Epstein;
the drawings were done by John Cordes, J. & R. Technical
Services, Inc. The editors were Herbert Waentig and
Laura Givner for McGraw-Hill Book Company and Verne A.
Stadtman and Margaret Cheney for the Carnegie Commission
on Higher Education. Frank Matonti supervised the production.*